# Best Bush & Coastal Walks of the Central Coast

By
Matt McClelland &
the Wildwalks Team

in association with

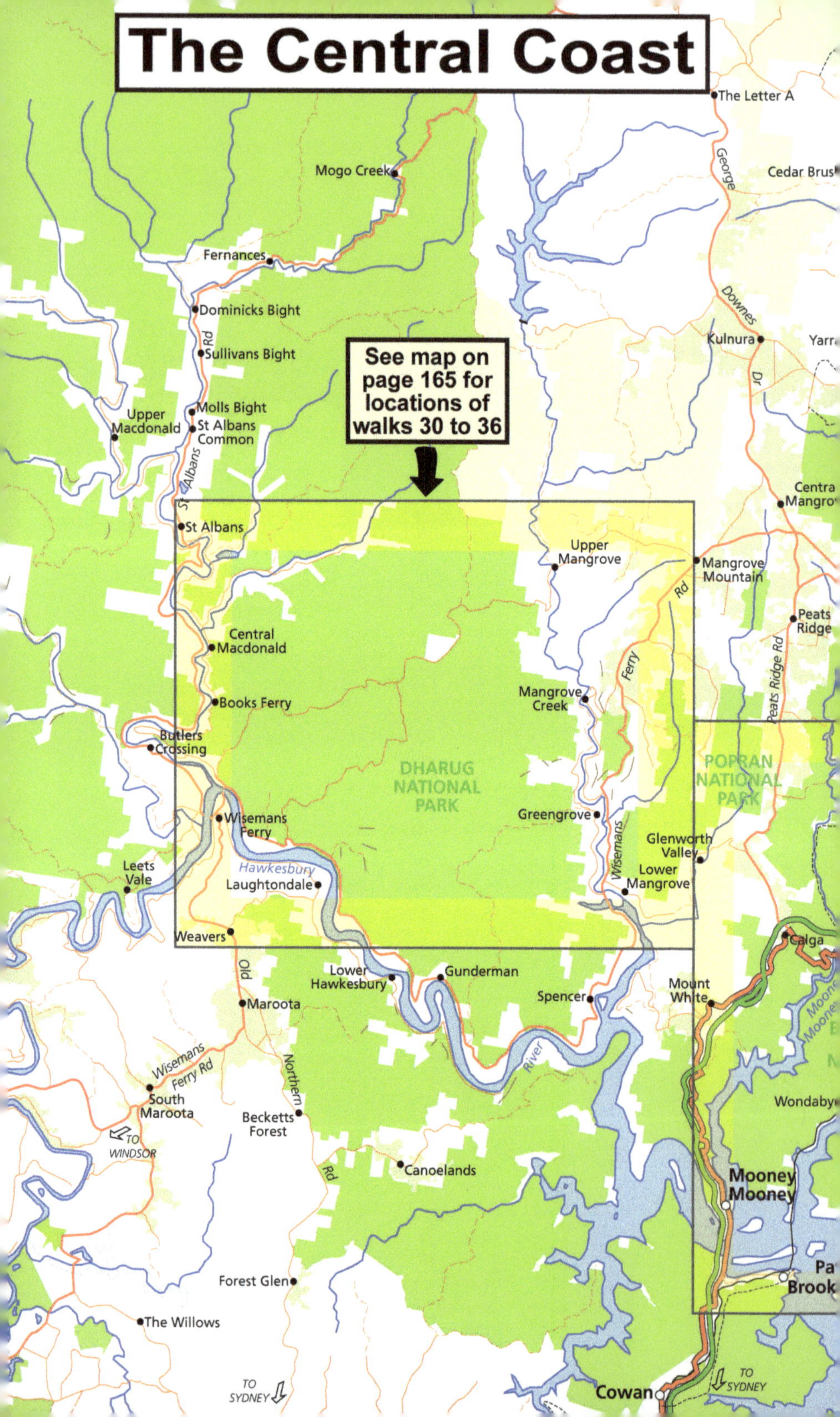

The Central Coast
See map on page 165 for locations of walks 30 to 36
The Letter A
George
Cedar Brus
Mogo Creek
Fernances
Dominicks Bight
Sullivans Bight
Rd
Molls Bight
Upper Macdonald
St Albans Common
St Albans
Downes
Dr
Kulnura
Yarr
Centra Mangro
St Albans
Upper Mangrove
Mangrove Mountain
Rd
Peats Ridge
Peats Ridge Rd
Central Macdonald
Books Ferry
Ferry
Mangrove Creek
Butlers Crossing
DHARUG NATIONAL PARK
POPRAN NATIONAL PARK
Wisemans Ferry
Greengrove
Wisemans
Glenworth Valley
Hawkesbury
Leets Vale
Laughtondale
Lower Mangrove
Weavers
Calga
Old
Lower Hawkesbury
Gunderman
Spencer
Mount White
Maroota
River
Wisemans Ferry Rd
South Maroota
Northern
Rd
Becketts Forest
TO WINDSOR
Wondaby
Canoelands
Mooney Mooney
Pa Brook
Forest Glen
The Willows
TO SYDNEY
Cowan
TO SYDNEY

Mandalong
TO NEWCASTLE, HUNTER REGION
Wyee Point
Windermere Park
Gwandalan
TO NEWCASTLE
Lemon Tree
Wyee Bay
Mannering Park
Mannering Lake
Chain Valley Bay
Highway
See map on page 163 for locations of walks 1 to 4
avensdale
Dooralong
Wyee
Doyalson North
Frazer Park
Pacific
Lake Munmorah
Doyalson
Freeway
Lake Munmorah
Motorway Link
Charmhaven
Budgewoi
Sparks
Rd
Little Jilliby
Budgewoi Lake
Warnervale
Highway
Gorokan
Jilliby
Kanwal
Toukley
Norahville
Wyong Creek
Korakoa
Wyongah
Norah Head
Wyong
Tuggerawong
Tacoma
Highway
Newcastle
Tuggerah
Tuggerah Lake
See map on page 164 for locations of walks 17 to 29
Kangy Angy
Titwood
Chittaway South
The Entrance
Pacific
Berkeley Vale
Wyong
Coast
Ourimbah
Rd
Long Jetty
Tumbi Umbi
Killarney Vale
Lisarow
Bateau Bay
See map on page 163 for locations of walks 5 to 11
Niagara Park
Narara
Central
Wyoming
Holgate
Forresters Beach
Matcham
Wamberal
Gosford
Springfield
Kariong
Erina
SOUTH PACIFIC OCEAN
Terrigal
Tascott
Brisbane Water
Brisbane Water Dr
Green Point
Yattalunga
Avoca Beach
Kincumber
Saratoga
Copacabana
Woy Woy
orsfield Bay
Bensville
McMasters Beach
BOUDDI NATIONAL PARK
Ettalong Beach
Hardys Bay
Umina
Killcare
Pretty Beach
See map on page 165 for locations of walks 12 to 16
Pearl Beach
River
N
0
10Km

To the next generation, particularly Eric and Laura.
I hope that we take great care of these natural places, and
I trust that you can pass them on to your children, in even better health.

---

Woodslane Press Pty Ltd
10 Apollo Street
Warriewood, NSW 2102
Australia
Email: info@woodslane.com.au
Tel: (02) 8445 2300 Web: www.woodslane.com.au

First published in Australia in 2010 by Woodslane Press, reprinted 2012
Copyright © 2010 Woodslane Press Pty Ltd; text, photographs and histograms © 2010 Matt McClelland and Wildwalks

All rights reserved. Apart from any fair dealing for the purposes of study, research or review, as permitted under Australian copyright law, no part of this publication may be reproduced, distributed, or transmitted in any other form or by any means, including photocopying, recording, or other electronic or mechanical methods, without the prior written permission of the publisher. For permission requests, write to the publisher, addressed "Attention: Permissions Coordinator", at the address above. Every effort has been made to obtain permissions relating to information reproduced in this publication. The information in this publication is based upon the current state of commercial and industry practice and the general circumstances as at the date of publication. No person shall rely on any of the contents of this publication and the publisher and the author expressly exclude all liability for direct and indirect loss suffered by any person resulting in any way from the use or reliance on this publication or any part of it. Any opinions and advice are offered solely in pursuance of the author's and publisher's intention to provide information, and have not been specifically sought.

National Library of Australia Cataloguing-in-Publication entry

McCelland, Matthew.

Best bush & coastal walks of the Central Coast: the full-colour guide to 36 fantastic walks / Matthew McClelland.

1st ed.

9781921606854 (pbk.)

Includes index.

Hiking--New South Wales--Central Coast--Guidebooks.
Walking--New South Wales--Central Coast--Guidebooks.
Central Coast (N.S.W.)--Description and travel.
796.5109944

Printed in Australia
Designed by Coral Lee
Main cover image: Broken Bay

Best Bush & Coastal
Walks of the
Central Coast

# Contents

**Regional map** ii-iii

**Introduction** 1

Walk grades and times 2

Track closures 2

Looking after the bush 3

Safety 3

**Walks at a glance** 6

**Best Bush & Coastal Walks of the Central Coast**

Around The Entrance 11

Around Gosford 35

Bouddi National Park 65

Brisbane Water National Park 85

Central West 119

Dharug National Park 143

**Location maps**

Around The Entrance and Gosford 163

Central West and Brisbane Water 164

Bouddi and Dharug National Parks 165

**Navigation and staying found** 166

**Map legend** 167

**Index** 168

**About the author and Wildwalks** 170

**Acknowledgements** 171

**Other books from Woodslane** 172

**Feedback** 174

# Introduction

The NSW Central Coast is a special place, blessed with some wonderful natural landscapes and many people flock to the coast in summer to enjoy the waterways and beaches. I trust that you will find great joy in discovering, exploring and sharing these walks.

A great way to ensure the ongoing health of our natural places is by encouraging more people to discover their significance. The National Parks and Wildlife Act of 1974 states that *"The purpose of reserving land as a national park is to identify, protect and conserve areas containing outstanding or representative ecosystems, natural or cultural features or landscapes or phenomena that provide opportunities for public appreciation and inspiration and sustainable visitor use and enjoyment....".*

The national parks system is one of the many good mechanisms we use to protect our diverse natural environments. I am incredibly thankful for the people who had the foresight to protect these places; they were not originally protected primarily for our recreation, but what a great privilege it is that we have the opportunity to visit, enjoy and marvel at these ancient landscapes. My hope is that, as you walk, you might find great encouragement from your experiences, and that this encouragement might lead to a deeper love for our natural and significant landscapes.

# Introduction

## Walk grades and times

Establishing grades and times can be a little tricky. These walks were initially graded using the AS 2156.1-2001, Australia's standard for track classification. To keep things simple, however, we have tweaked the grades to help keep a consistent feel for this book series. You'll soon figure out whether your own pace is faster or slower than what's shown in this book. The walk times do not include extra time for rests, side trips or safety margins, please always allow extra time.

Some general rules of thumb when looking at walk grades in this book:

**Easy:** Suitable for people new to bushwalking; take care with children

**Medium:** Suitable for people who walk occasionally

**Hard:** Steep sections, or requires particular attention to safety and navigation skills; these are for people who walk regularly

**Very hard:** For experienced walkers; a high level of fitness, bushcraft and navigational skills are required

Hills can really slow things down. A relatively level 6 kilometre walk will take half the time of a similar length walk that climbs and descends 600 metres (Google "Naismith's rule" to learn more).

## Track closures

All tracks are susceptible to closures for many reasons. Help park managers and save your frustration by checking for track and park closures information prior to setting out. Information about closures on National Park estate can be found at www.npws.nsw.gov.au_or by phoning 1300 361 967. Forests NSW (T 1300 655687 ) and Gosford City Council (T 4325 8222) post some closure information but it is best to call and check, especially if you are travelling some distance. Unless you can find out otherwise, the safest option is to **assume parks are closed on days of total fire bans**. All walks in this book fall in the *Greater Sydney Region* fire area. Current ratings and fire bans can be found at www.rfs.nsw.gov.au or by phoning T 1800 679737.

## Looking after the bush

Chances are, you already know the basics. As a quick recap please remember to: take your rubbish, stay on the tracks, don't pick wildflowers, don't break branches off trees and don't blaze new trails. If nature calls and there are no toilets, bury your waste in a hole 15 cm deep and at least 100 metres away from any water source. Leave your dog at home, and if you're lucky enough to see a wild animal, be still and let it be (please do not feed it).

Avoid lighting fires, but if you do need to, use an existing fire place. Only light a fire if you are confident there are no total fire bans in place (neither park nor RFS bans). Make sure the fire is cold before leaving it unattended. In total fire bans you cannot use a camping stove. In summer be prepared with food that does not need cooking.

## Safety and comfort

Although bushwalkers have died walking in the Central Coast region, most serious problems can easily be avoided. Following are some ideas to help make your time out bush safer and more enjoyable. It is not possible to teach all that is needed here, however, and if you are not an experienced walker, then consider finding someone who is or consider joining a walking club. Walking with a competent bushwalker will help build your own skills, comfort and safety levels.

- Be confident enough to **pull out if things aren't right**. It doesn't take much for a minor incident to turn major, especially if you are ill or the weather is not favourable. If things look wrong, postpone your walk for another day.
- **Choose walks that are suitable** for you and your walking buddies. Walkers with heart, circulatory or breathing difficulties should be particularly cautious.

# Introduction

- **Keep well back from cliff edges** and keep a close eye on children.
- **Carry plenty of drinking water.** Sadly, you can't rely on the availability or quality of water on many of these walks. Avoid walking on hot days, consider resting in a shady spot in the middle of warmer days and be well hydrated before you start. On hot summer days you can lose around 3 litres of water per hour during activity. Generally you want to carry at least one litre of water per person for every two hours of walking, but on hot days carry more. Water is heavy, but critical for life.

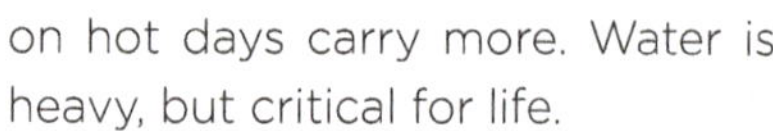

- **Eat well**. Walking in the bush is a key time to eat well. Take some time to plan your food and snacks. Eating good food with friends in the bush is much better than the fatigue from hunger. Fresh fruit will last, if packed well.
- **Wear sensible shoes.** Choose comfortable and sturdy shoes; avoid using new shoes on a long walk (at least carry your old shoes with you). Look after your feet; if you feel a hotspot, take the time to prevent the blister before it grows.
- **Keep an eye on the weather.** The weather can change quickly. If you're walking for more than a few hours, or if rain is forecast, pack some wet weather and warm clothing. Visit www.bom.gov.au for forecasts.
- **Slip Slop Slap** Seek Slide. Slip on a shirt, slop on sunscreen, slap on a hat, seek shade, and slide on the sunnies. Visit www.cancer.org.au to learn more about protecting yourself from the sun.
- **Carry and know how to use a first-aid kit.** A remote area first-aid kit from an outdoor store is a great idea. Training in first aid, especially remote area first aid is very worthwhile, and potentially lifesaving. Make sure you and your friends are carrying any regularly taken personal medication. If anyone in your group has asthma, severe allergies or other life threatening conditions, make sure a few people understand

the signs and the appropriate management plan. Know how and when to apply a pressure immobilisation bandage and how to help a person who is unconscious. A good insect repellent can help relieve you of a few critters such as ticks, leeches and mozzies.

- **Walk in a group**. Some people enjoy walking alone, but it is much safer to walk with other people. If you choose to walk alone, then take extra precautions to deal with the significant increased risk.
- **Tell some where you are going**. Even on short walks, always make sure someone responsible knows where you're going, when to expect you back, and what to do if you are late returning.
- **Carry a mobile phone**. In an emergency dial 112 (only works on digital mobile phones; dial 000 from any other type of phone); this gives you the best chance of talking to the emergency services. Be ready to explain where you are and what help you need. Even a second hand digital phone with no sim card can make an emergency call; if you don't own a phone, ask a friend for their old one. Charge and conserve your battery.
- **Carry a PLB.** Seriously consider buying, borrowing or hiring a Personal Locator Beacon (PLB - somctimes referred to as an EPIRB) or another satellite based emergency beacon, such as SPOT. These devices call for help in a life-threatening situation. They work even when your mobile phone does not. A PLB offers a fast and reliable way to attract help; other devices like SPOT may be a bit slower, but offer additional functionality. They may sound expensive, but only until you need one. Trigger your PLB if there is a threat of grave and imminent danger, and there are no other reasonable means of communication (ie: try your phone first). I always carry a beacon with me in the bush, even on short walks. Help will come, but it will take time; be prepared to wait for several hours, or even overnight.

See page 166 for further information on navigation, not getting lost and getting found if you do.

# Walks at a glance

| | Walk | Page | Distance (km) | Time | Grad |
|---|---|---|---|---|---|
| **Around The Entrance** | | | | | |
| 1 | Munmorah Coastal | 12 | 3.3 one way | 1 hr 30 mins | Hard |
| 2 | Norah Head Lighthouse Loop | 16 | 2.5 circuit | 1 hr | Mediu |
| 3 | Redgum Trail | 22 | 3.4 circuit | 1 hr 15 mins | Mediu |
| 4 | Lillypilly Loop Trail | 26 | 3.6 circuit | 1 hr 15 mins | Mediu |
| 5 | Wyrrabalong Coast Walking Track | 29 | 3.8 one way | 1 hr 30 mins | Mediu |
| **Around Gosford** | | | | | |
| 6 | Ouraka Point Loop | 36 | 2.1 circuit | 1 hr 15 mins | Mediu |
| 7 | Ironbark and Flannel Flower Circuit | 40 | 2.1 circuit | 1 hr | Mediu |
| 8 | Rainforest walk to Nurrunga | 44 | 2.2 one way | 1 hr | Mediu |
| 9 | Gosford to Lisarow | 48 | 11.3 one way | 4 hrs 30 mins | Mediu |
| 10 | Katandra Reserve Explorer | 54 | 5.3 circuit | 2 hrs 45 mins | Mediu |
| 11 | Kincumber to Terrigal | 60 | 4.5 one way | 2 hrs | Mediu |
| **Bouddi National Park** | | | | | |
| 12 | Box Head | 66 | 3.1 return | 2 hrs | Mediu |
| 13 | Bullimah Outlook | 69 | 2.3 return | 1 hr 15 mins | Mediu |
| 14 | Gerrin Point Circuit | 73 | 5.2 circuit | 2 hrs 30 mins | Mediu |
| 15 | Little Beach | 78 | 1.2 return | 30 mins | Easy |
| 16 | Bouddi Coastal Walk | 80 | 8.1 one way | 5 hrs | Mediu |

| Café | Water access | Ascent (m) | Descent (m) | Highlights |
|---|---|---|---|---|
| - | Yes | 100 | 100 | Wildflowers, coast views, Frazer Beach |
| Nearby | Yes | 70 | 70 | Lighthouse, coast views, rock pool |
| - | - | 50 | 50 | Angophora forest, Tuggerah Lake views |
| - | Yes | 60 | 60 | Tuggerah Lake shore, diverse forest |
| Nearby | Yes | 70 | 75 | Coast Views, picnic areas, beaches |
| Nearby | - | 140 | 140 | Ouraka Point Lookout, dry forests |
| - | - | 110 | 110 | Lookouts, varied forests, picnic areas |
| - | - | 200 | 50 | Varied forest, sculptures, lookouts, picnic area |
| Start | - | 480 | 460 | District views, wildflowers, picnic areas |
| - | - | 350 | 350 | Strangler Fig trees, Seymour Pond, lookout |
| - | - | 220 | 220 | Rock formations, picnic area, lookout |
| - | - | 130 | 130 | Views from Box Head |
| - | - | 100 | 100 | Views from Bullimah Outlook, ridge walking |
| - | Yes | 300 | 300 | View from Gerrin Point, beaches and coastline |
| - | Yes | 50 | 50 | Little Beach, picnic area |
| - | Yes | 370 | 410 | Coastal views, shipwreck, beaches, botany |

# Walks at a glance

| Walk | Page | Distance (km) | Time | Grade |
|---|---|---|---|---|

## Brisbane Water National Park

| Walk | Page | Distance (km) | Time | Grade |
|---|---|---|---|---|
| 17 Mt Ettalong | 86 | 1.4 return | 30 mins | Easy |
| 18 Patonga to Pearl Beach | 88 | 4.2 one way | 1 hr 30 mins | Mediur |
| 19 Little Wobby to Woy Woy | 92 | 16.1 one way | 6 hrs 30 mins | Very Ha |
| 20 Staples Lookout to Mount Wondabyne Circuit | 98 | 10.8 circuit | 4 hrs 30 mins | Mediu |
| 21 Staples Lookout to Kariong Brook Falls | 102 | 5.7 return | 2 hrs 30 mins | Mediur |
| 22 Pindar Cave | 104 | 11.5 return | 4 hrs 30 mins | Hard |
| 23 Bulgandry Engravings | 107 | 0.8 return | 20 mins | Easy |
| 24 Girrakool Loop | 110 | 1.4 circuit | 45 mins | Mediur |
| 25 Piles Creek Circuit | 114 | 4.1 circuit | 2 hrs | Mediur |

## Central West

| Walk | Page | Distance (km) | Time | Grade |
|---|---|---|---|---|
| 26 Bellbird Trail | 120 | 3.3 circuit | 1 hr 15 mins | easy |
| 27 Strickland Falls and Cabbage Tree Loop | 124 | 3 circuit | 1 hr 30 mins | easy |
| 28 Somersby Falls | 128 | 0.4 return | 20 mins | Mediur |
| 29 Popran Creek from Peats Ridge Road | 132 | 2.5 return | 1 hr 15 mins | Mediur |
| 30 Ironbark Road to Glenworth Valley | 134 | 10 return | 4 hrs 15 mins | Hard |
| 31 Emerald Pool Circuit | 138 | 10.8 circuit | 4 hrs 15 mins | Mediur |

## Dharug National Park

| Walk | Page | Distance (km) | Time | Grade |
|---|---|---|---|---|
| 32 Dubbo Gully to Upper Mangrove Cemetery | 144 | 7.2 return | 3 hrs 15 mins | Mediur |
| 33 Dubbo Gully and 10-mile Hollow Circuit | 148 | 24.3 circuit | 2 Days | Hard |
| 34 Devines Hill and Finch's Line Circuit | 152 | 9.9 circuit | 4 hrs 30 mins | Medium |
| 35 11km (Mill Creek) Circuit | 156 | 8.2 circuit | 4 hrs 15 mins | Hard |
| 36 Grass Tree Circuit | 160 | 1.7 circuit | 1 hr | Medium |

| Café | Water access | Ascent (m) | Descent (m) | Highlights |
| --- | --- | --- | --- | --- |
| - | - | 30 | 30 | Views, angophora forest |
| Yes | Yes | 180 | 180 | Water views, beaches, villages, diverse forest |
| End | Yes | 590 | 600 | Water views, waterfalls, remoteness |
| - | Sidetrip | 340 | 340 | View from Mt Wondabyne, rocky outcrops |
| - | Yes | 230 | 230 | Falls, sandstone rocks, grass trees |
| - | - | 490 | 490 | Pindar Cave, district views, remoteness |
| - | - | 20 | 20 | Aboriginal engravings, wildflowers |
| - | Yes | 60 | 60 | Lookouts, waterfalls, Aboriginal engravings |
| - | Yes | 300 | 300 | Lookouts, waterfalls, caves, suspension bridge |
| - | - | 90 | 90 | Birds, diverse forest, creek crossings |
| - | - | 220 | 220 | Rock formations, waterfall (after rain), ferns |
| - | Yes | 40 | 40 | Waterfalls, picnic areas, forest |
| - | Yes | 190 | 190 | Sandy Creek, moist forest |
| Yes | - | 490 | 490 | Views, varied forest, Glenworth Valley |
| - | Yes | 350 | 350 | Emerald Pool, varied forests, outcrops |
| - | - | 450 | 450 | Historic cemetery, roads and farms |
| - | - | 1120 | 1120 | Historic cemetery, roads, bridges, forests |
| - | - | 550 | 550 | Historic road, river views, sandstone cuttings |
| - | - | 630 | 630 | Grass trees, sandstone cliffs, rugged country |
| - | - | 110 | 110 | Grass trees, sandstone formations, forest |

# Around The Entrance

Near many of the premium tourist destinations on the Central Coast, the walks in this chapter provide a wonderful way for locals and visitors to connect with the land and discover a series of rich and diverse coastal environments. These walks are scattered along the narrow coastal strip between Forresters Beach and Catherine Hill Bay, bounded by the South Pacific Ocean to the east and the Tuggerah Lakes system to the west.

Munmorah State Conservation Area, which really shows its vibrant personality in spring when wildflowers are in full bloom, is explored in the first walk. Beyond this, the park still has much to offer visitors with spectacular sea cliffs, long sandy beaches, palm forests, picnic areas and two great camp grounds. The next walk focuses on Norah Head Lighthouse Reserve, a small reserve protecting a pocket of bushland and the lighthouse, which was opened on 15th November 1903 and is still in use today. This reserve showcases local marine history and provides many grand coastal views. Wyrrabalong National Park protects a number of important environments including the last significant stand of littoral rainforest on the Central Coast. These walks help you explore the coastal cliffs and the majestic *Angophora costata* (Sydney Red Gum) forest.

# 1 Munmorah Coast Track

Starting from Campbell Drive, this walk follows the Geebung and Grass Tree tracks to Frazer Beach, with an optional side trip to Wybung Head. Geebung Track leads you through low heath and past a few sweeping ocean views, as well as great wildflower displays in spring and summer. The side trip to Wybung Head follows a dirt road, and the views are well worth the detour. Grass Tree Track is overgrown and unclear in places as it makes its way down to Frazer Beach.

## At a glance

**Grade:** Hard

**Time:** 1 hr 30 mins

**Distance:** 3.3 km one way

**Ascent/descent:** 100 metres ascent / descent

**Conditions:** Limited shade, best on clear but cooler days

**Getting there:**

**Car:** Turn off the Pacific Hwy and follow Blue Wren Dr for 1.7 km then turn left and follow Campbell Dr for 800 m to find a small car park. The walk finishes at end of Frazer Beach Rd (found further along Campbell Dr). Either organise a second car or allow extra time to walk back to the start.

**GPS of start:** -33.1954, 151.6016

**GPS of end:** -33.1878, 151.622

Frazer Beach

## Walk directions

1 From Campbell Drive, head south around the locked gate, though the clearing and then follow the *Coast Track* sign along the management trail. After about 350 metres, the management trail ends and you cross a small creek using a timber boardwalk. Head up a series of timber steps (where the track is lined with timber for a short time) and across a small clearing. The track then leads back through tall dense heath for about 200 metres. Veer left and up the wide ridge through the low heath, with wide district views behind, then near the top of the hill (as Birdie Beach comes into view on the right), and just after a significant left-hand bend, you'll come to the first of the ocean views along Birdie Beach. The view south is over Red Ochre Beach then along Birdie Beach. You can also see past Bird Island to Norah Head in the distance.

2 Continue north along the wide track that soon leads into taller heath. You'll soon pass another view into an un-named bay (on the right) and then continue through the tall heath for a while. Not long before Wybung Head Road, turn right at a 'Y' intersection then through a clearing. Head around the locked gate to the turning area and car park on Wybung Head Road.

3 Turn right and walk along the road for 60 metres.

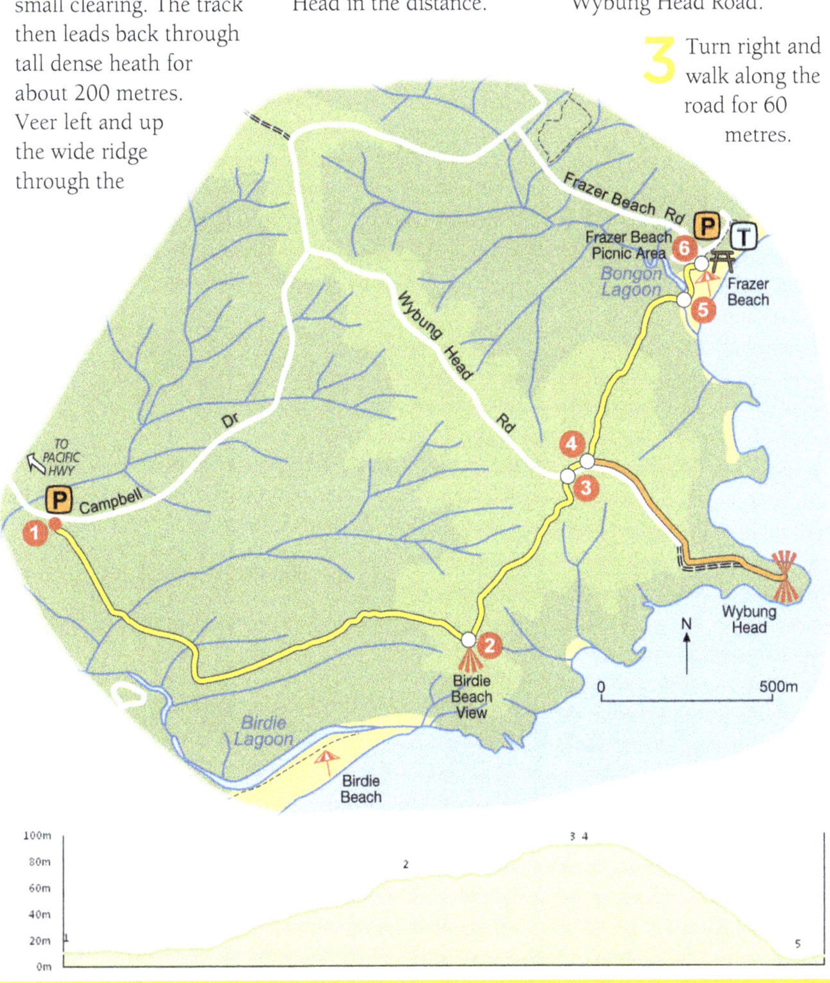

Bongon Lagoon

Just before the right-hand bend, you'll find an intersection with the faint Grass Tree Track on the left, just after the heath becomes taller. (Remember this point if you are taking the optional side trip to Wybung Head).

The Geebung Track

**4** Follow the faint Grass Tree Track north over a small rise and through the dense vegetation. Soon the vegetation becomes shorter and the track becomes clearer. There are some distant ocean views as you meander gently downhill for a while before the track becomes steeper and eroded in places. Try to follow the main track, and avoid the smaller side tracks that have been created. As you approach the beach, you'll enter a forest of taller trees and finally reach Frazer Beach, just at the bottom end of Bongon Lagoon. This beach is a popular swimming area with a patrol service provided during Christmas, Easter and April school holidays.

**5** Tend left along the sand, keeping the lagoon to the left, then tend right up to the lower car park, past the picnic shelters and tables, to the end of Frazer Beach Road. The picnic area has wide ocean views over the beach and there's a nearby amenities block (toilet and showers) plus an emergency telephone.

## Walk variation - side trip to end of Wybung Head

This side trip adds about 1.5 kilometres to the walk, but is well worth the extra time. From point 4 head along Wybung Head Road towards the ocean. Soon after passing a sweeping right-hand bend, the walk comes to a car park and the end of the road. Go through the locked gate and follow the management trail down the hill to find the wide ocean views. Continue along the trail at the top of an unfenced cliff, to a grassy clearing in the middle of a narrow saddle. A narrower track continues to the end of the point, where the heath suddenly opens up at the top of an unfenced cliff and view across the ocean. Wybung is a local Aboriginal word meaning 'Dangerous Sea'. The headland provides clear views up and down the coast and is a popular whale watching area.

View North from Wybung Head

## Make a day of it

Whilst in the area, you may enjoy a drive to the end of Snapper Point Road to see the large Snapper Point Sea Cave, and walk along the short management trail to Snapper Point. Birdie Beach is a popular area for visitors and the more secluded walk to Timber Beach is a good opportunity to explore a quieter section of the park. You can make a weekend of it by camping at either Frazer or Freemans camping grounds.

# 2 Norah Head Lighthouse Loop

This wonderful loop walk, with a great variety of scenery, takes in the forest of the Norah Head Nature Trail, the merchant navy memorial and Norah Head lighthouse before returning via the shoreline. There are plenty of impressive coastline views and the opportunity to explore the rockshelf below the lighthouse. On weekends, you can also join a tour of the lighthouse (every half hour from 1000-1330).

## At a glance

**Grade:** Medium (the rockshelf will present extra difficulty)

**Time:** 1 hr

**Distance:** 2.5 km circuit

**Ascent/descent:** 70 metres ascent/descent

**Conditions:** All seasons. Only consider attempting the rockshelf at low tide and low seas

**Getting there:**

**Bus:** Catch Busways route 79 from Wyong station to Lake Haven shopping centre then route 90 to the intersection of Bungary Rd and Maitland St - turn left and walk along Maitland St (becomes Bush St) to the Bush St Reserve (hourly services)

**Car:** Drive to Bush St Reserve, near the junction of Young St and Bush St, Norah Head

**GPS of start/end:** -33.2804, 151.5694

## Walk directions

1 Walk from the car park at the Bush Street Reserve across the park for 90 metres to the information board and track head at the back corner of the park.

2 Walk through the timber barricade past the *Headland Nature Trail* sign. After spending a while winding through the bush your track will intersect with another, close to a fenced lookout platform.

3 Veer left at the intersection and walk 15 metres to the Headland lookout platform.

4 From the lookout, walk back to the previous intersection and turn left, following the *Nature Trail* arrow left through the bush. After passing over a small timber bridge you will reach the lighthouse car park.

5 Head through the car park and to the left, then cross Bush Street to the Merchant Mariners memorial and lookout. There are some plaques in the footpath and in rocks at the memorial with information about merchant ships and lives lost during World War II.

6 Take the footpath towards the lighthouse past an information board. After 120 metres you will

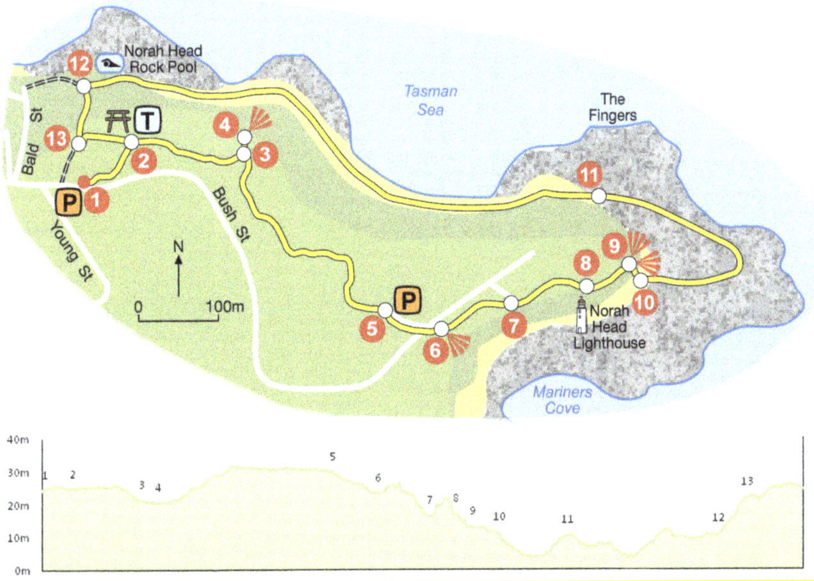

Norah Head Lighthouse

arrive at the corner of the lighthouse cottage yard (the lighthouse can be booked for accommodation, T 1300 132 975, with the grounds available for weddings and events, T 4396 4102).

7 From the corner of the yard, walk past the lighthouse cottages for 100 metres to the gate beside the lighthouse. Established in 1903 this was converted from kerosene to electric power in 1961. Tours are available on weekends every half hour from 1000-1330.

8 Head down the hill towards the ocean where, after 80 metres you'll find a viewing point at the top a set of steps offering views up and down the coastline.

9 Walk down the timber steps to the beach at the bottom.

10 At the beach turn left. There's the option to spend some time exploring the rock platform here, but make sure conditions are safe beforehand. Keeping the ocean to the right, walk around the headland until you reach the southern end of Lighthouse Beach.

11 Still keeping the ocean to the right, head towards the rock platform at the north end

of the beach. Head up the steps and along the footpath with the metal handrail, around the headland and past the ocean pool to the bottom of the concrete steps, just below the toilet block.

**12** Walk up the steps away from the ocean pool, past the toilet block and along the footpath for 90 metres to an intersection signposted *Cabbage Tree Harbour Rock Pool path, Bush St.*

**13** Turn left – soon you will reach an open grassy area. Turn right and find the information board and track head at the back of the park. You are now back at waypoint 2. Retrace your earlier steps across the park and back to the car park.

Wyrrabalong Coast Walking Track

# 3 Redgum trail

Looping through the Sydney Red gums in Wyrrabalong National Park, this walk takes you under twisted trees leaning over the track, creating great scenery and atmosphere. Two lookout platforms along the way provide views over the surrounding areas and Tuggerah Lake. Much of the walk is on sandy tracks.

## At a glance

**Grade:** : Medium

**Time:** 1 hrs 15 mins

**Distance:** 3.4 km circuit

**Ascent/descent:** 50 metres ascent/ descent

**Conditions:** All seasons

**Getting there:**

**Car:** Drive to the Wyrrabalong National Park signposted car park on the Central Coast Hwy, aka Wilfred Barret Dr, about 7 km north of The Entrance bridge

**GPS of start/end:** -33.2937, 151.5466

## Walk directions

1 Walk from the car park through the timber fence and past an information board, following the sandy management trail. After 60 metres you will reach the intersection of the *Red Gum Trail* and the *Burrawang Walking Track*.

2 Follow the *Red Gum Trail* arrow to the right and along the sandy track. You will climb a little through a series of bends, passing a couple more *Red Gum Trail* signs. Turn left when you arrive at the intersection with the *Wetland Trail*, dropping through a gully and up the other side. When you pass a *Red Gum Forest* information board, continue another 300 metres to find a wooden lookout platform with views to the north and northeast.

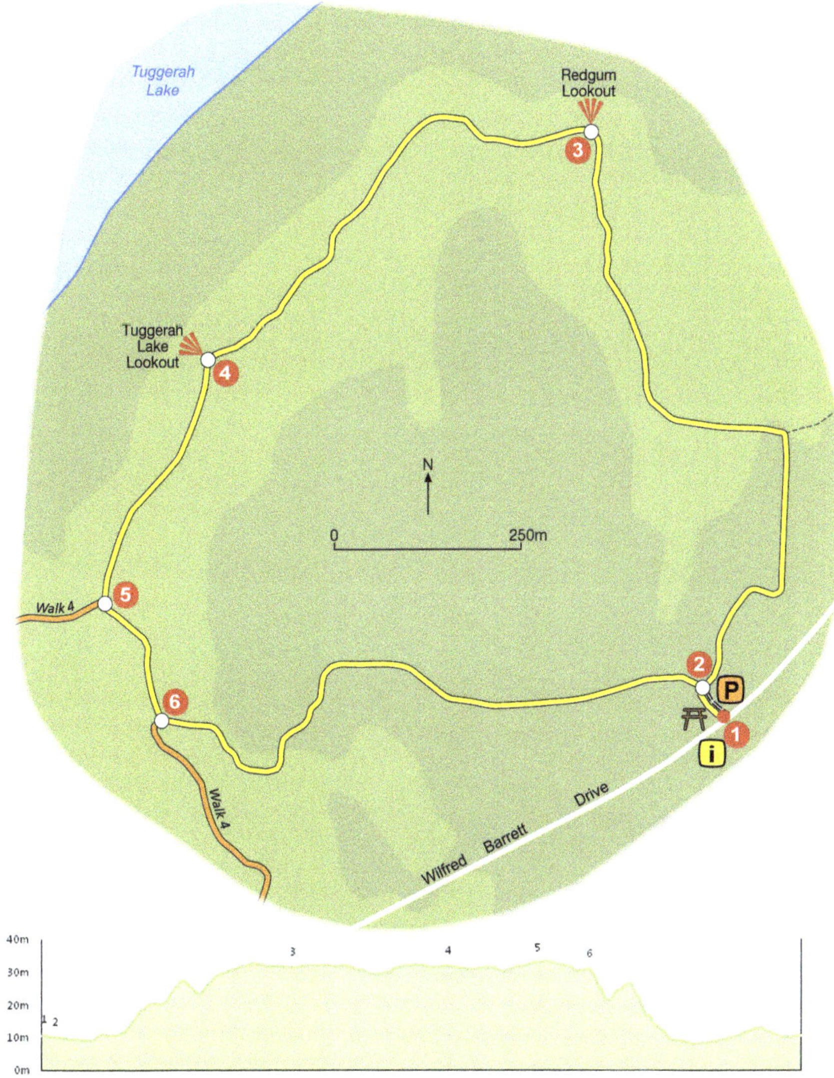

**3** Continue along the sandy bush track through the forest and around to the left. You'll have glimpses of Tuggerah Lake to the right and the ocean to the left for a while, until you reach another fenced wooden lookout platform with more views west over Tuggerah Lake.

**4** Walk on through the forest for 400 metres to the intersection with the *Lilly Pilly Loop Trail*.

**5** Turn left, following the *Lilly Pilly Loop Trail*, down through a gully and some more forest before coming to an intersection with the *Burrawang Walking Track*.

**6** Again turn left, through the forest and some thick vegetation, passing a *Burrawang Walking Track* signpost. Eventually you will reach the signposted intersection with the *Red Gum Trail* (you are now back at waypoint 2). Veer right and follow the trail back to the car park.

# 4 Lillypilly Loop Trail

Passing through a variety of forest scenery, this walk includes some rainforest, dominated by cabbage palms and other trees in Wyrrabalong National Park. There are some remarkable views across Tuggerah Lake, and parts of the track feature twisted Sydney red gums and the shorter palm-like Burrawang (a species of cycad). Much of the walk is on sandy tracks, with sections of timber boarding to control erosion.

## At a glance

**Grade:** Medium

**Time:** 1 hrs 15 mins

**Distance:** 3.6 km circuit

**Ascent/descent:** 60 metres ascent/ descent

**Conditions:** All seasons

**Getting there:**

**Car:** Drive to the *Wyrrabalong National Park* car park on the Central Coast Hwy (aka Wilfred Barret Dr), about 5.5 km north of The Entrance bridge

**GPS of start/end:** -33.3006, 151.5329

## Walk directions

1 Walk around the gate and past the information board and *Lilly Pilly Loop Trail* sign to follow the management trail up the hill. After about 80 metres the trail bends left towards an intersection marked with a *Lilly Pilly Loop Link Trail* sign.

2 Continue straight, heading along the ridge, through relatively dry forest and down into moist littoral rainforest. The path will meander through here and past a Rainforests information board to a vista at the edge of Tuggerah Lake.

3 Head right along the lake edge. You will pass through some drier forest with sections of erosion control timber boards on the track, reaching the intersection with the *Red Gum Trail* in just over a kilometre.

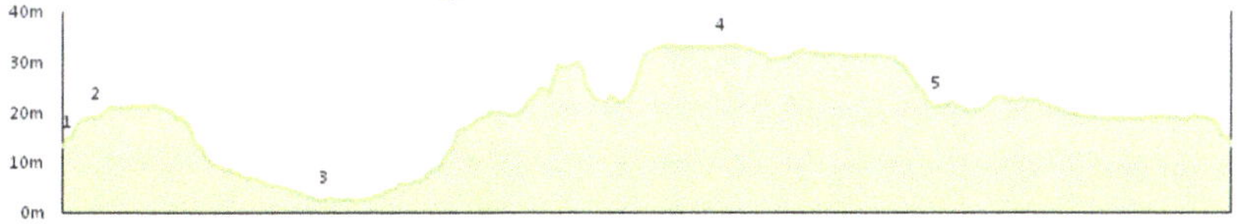

**4** Follow the arrow on the *Lilly Pilly Loop Trail* sign to the right, heading down through a gully and winding through some more pleasant forest for a short distance. At the intersection with the *Burrawang Walking Track*, veer right and up the hill. After a while the track descends, treading over more sections of timber boards before turning right at the intersection with *Lilly Pilly Loop Link Trail*.

**5** This section of the track meanders through a mixture of littoral and drier rainforest. After a while, you will head through some thick, vine-covered vegetation to an intersection marked with another *Lilly Pilly Loop Link Trail* sign (you are now back at waypoint 2). Turn left and follow the sandy management trail back to the car park.

# 5 Wyrrabalong Coast Walking Track

Explore the ridge along the southern section of Wyrrabalong National Park in this walk, wandering along the thin strip of coastal forest, with views of the coastline from many vantage points along the way. The two main lookouts, Crackneck and Wyrrabalong, have stunning views and would be great spots to stop for a picnic lunch.

## At a glance

**Grade:** Medium

**Time:** 1 hr 30 mins

**Distance:** 3.8 km one way

**Ascent/descent:** 180 metres ascent / 70 metres descent

**Conditions:** Views are great on sunny days

**Getting there:**
**Bus**: The Red Bus Services 21/22/23 get you to Gosford Station and either end of this walk at least every hour, 7 days (21 gets you closest to the start)

**Car:** Street parking at the intersection of Bateau Bay Rd and Moronga St, Bateau Bay; walk starts near the Entrance of Blue Lagoon Beach Resort

**GPS of start:** -33.3781, 151.4842

**GPS of end:** -33.4053, 151.4745

# 5 Wyrrabalong Coast Walking Track

## Walk directions

1 From the entrance to the Blue Lagoon Beach Resort, head behind the wooden fence and alongside Bateau Bay Rd (keeping the road to the right). After a short distance the track swings away from the road and through the trees. Turn right at an intersection near a view overlooking the caravan park and keep moving along the main track to the picnic area, which has beautiful views along the coast (there are free electric BBQs here and takeaway food nearby). Head to the top of the wooden beach access steps, beside which you will find an intersection.

2 Continue straight on and across the picnic area to some seats and the ocean lookout on the left. From here head past a fenced lookout to just before a Y intersection at the end of the picnic area.

3 Take the right track past the *Wyrrabalong National Park Service Trail Walkers Only* sign, initially keeping the concrete path to the left. You will pass through a narrow strip of forest and go past a number of lookouts with clear views out to sea. After a while, the track leads you to another picnic area.

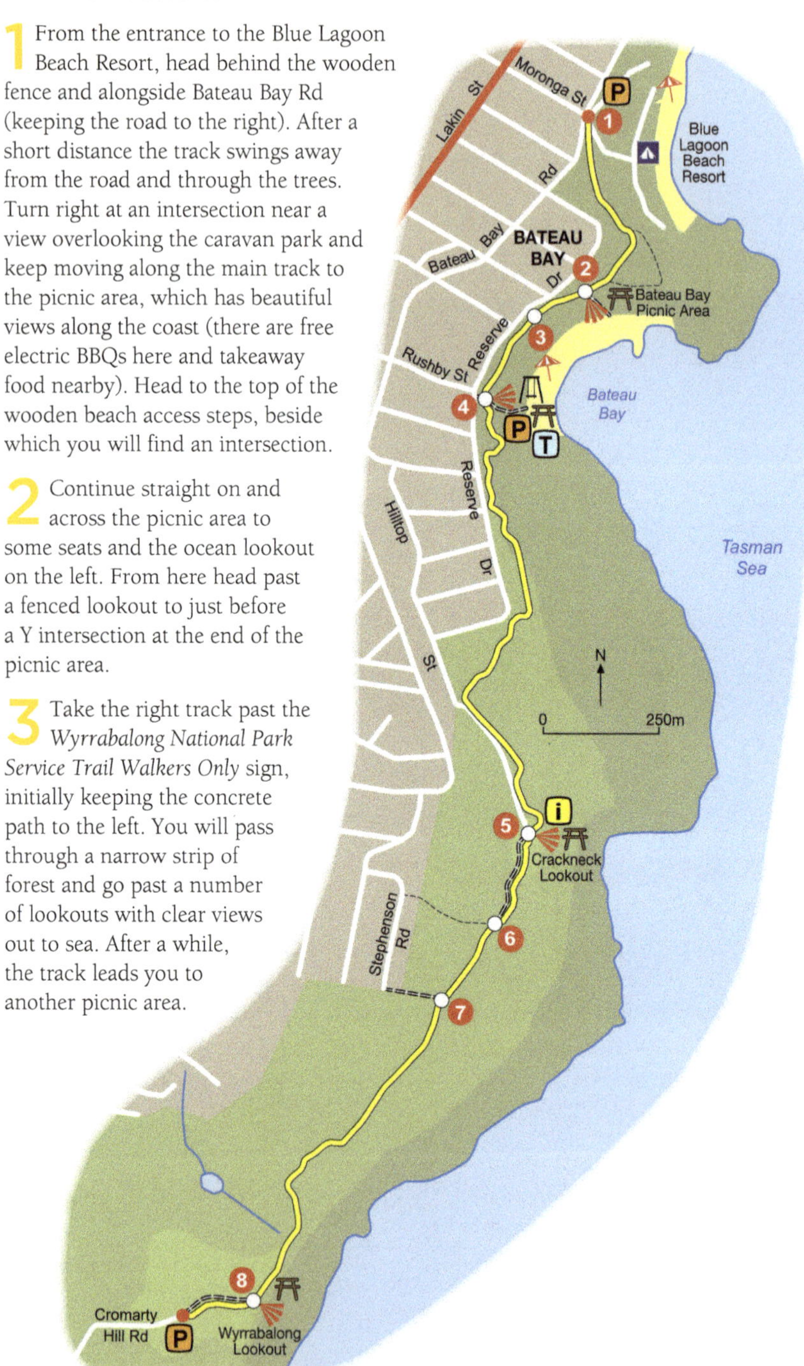

Walk across to the junction at the Coast Track signpost (next to Reserve Drive).

4 Keeping Reserve Drive to the right, follow the Coast Track, climbing gently past a number of informal side tracks (which lead to more ocean viewing spots or the nearby road). About 400 metres later you will come to the middle of another large grassy clearing with more ocean views. From here veer left along the bush track, heading back into the bush. Walk on past a bench seat with a commemorative plaque and another track to the right (which goes to the nearby street). The track is edged with timber for about 250 metres before turning left and running parallel with Hilltop St. After about 300 metres of boardwalk, climb for another 250 metres up some wooden steps to Crackneck Lookout, next to which there is a hang gliding launch spot.

5 From the lookout follow the fence around to the other side of the car park and take the old Coast Track management trail toward Wyrrabalong Lookout. Take the right-hand branch at the Y intersection to another view then continue along the main trail until it ends in a small sandy clearing.

6 Take the track marked with timber posts for about 15 metres then turn left at the intersection. Head through more bush with plenty of grass trees to another junction (with the track on the right leading up to Stephenson Road).

7 Turn left and follow the short sandstone wall-lined track passing a Coastal Heathlands information board to continue along the top of a ridge. Head down the long set of metal stairs, then through a section of thick

heath before emerging briefly to more ocean views. Keep walking past a few more occasional ocean views then climb several sets of wooden steps up to Wyrrabalong Lookout. This is a good spot for a lunch stop.

8 Turn right and walk across the grassy area, past a trig point, and follow the management trail between the communications tower and satellite dish. There are great views over Forresters Beach from the concrete platform on top of the building, next to the tower. Head down the hill and around a gate signposted *Wyrrabalong National Park* boundary, to the end of Cromarty Hill Road. At the end of this walk it is possible to walk back to the start along the beach and rocky coast. However, sections are very narrow and must only be attempted at low tide and when the sea conditions will allow a safe passage. If at all unsure of the conditions the return options are to catch a bus or taxi, or simply retrace your steps. To get to the Forester Beach shops [on the intersection of Central Coast Highway and Forresters Beach Road] walk along Cromarty Hill Road from the end of the walk for about 850 metres, turn right and follow Forresters Beach Road for another 450 metres.)

# Around Gosford

Near many of the premium tourist destinations on the Central Coast, the Nestled among the suburbs around Gosford are a series of reserves providing a great chance for people to get-away-from-it-all so close to home. Managed under Gosford City's Coastal Open Space System, these three reserves provide a great place to explore, close to home and work.

Rumbalara Reserve is nestled on the eastern side of the Gosford CBD, providing many walking tracks, picnic area and lookouts. The council has tastefully integrated sculptural art into the walking experiences and provides some well maintained facilities at the top of the hill. Katandra Reserve extends northeast from Rumbalara Reserve and is home to the large St John Lookout picnic area and of course the lookout itself. In the valley below the lookout is a temperate rainforest nurturing some spectacular strangler fig trees and the bird life around Seymour Pond. Kincumber Mountain is southeast of Gosford CBD and is well known for the lovely Honeman's Picnic area. This reserve showcases some fantastic grass trees and rock formations, including some large sandstone caves.

# 6 Ouraka Point loop

On this walk you will explore some of the scenic highlights of the lower section of the Rumbalara Reserve, covering a variety of vegetation, from quite dry eucalypt forest through to rainforest. The tracks are well formed, with a lot of steps in the steeper sections, making the climbs and descents a little easier. This is a great way to take in some of the Rumbalara scenery and a short side trip takes you to a sculpture of Charles Sturt. The easy access from Gosford train station makes it handy for those using public transport.

## At a glance

**Grade:** Medium

**Time:** 1 hrs 15 mins

**Distance:** 2.1 km circuit

**Ascent/descent:** 140 metres ascent/descent

**Conditions:** All seasons

**Getting there:**

**Train:** Gosford Station

**Car:** Drive to the Rumbalara EEC at the end of Donnison St, Gosford

**GPS of start/end:** -33.4277, 151.3477

## Finding the track

From Gosford train station head out the main eastern exit and cross the Pacific Highway using the glass-covered footbridge. On the other side of the bridge, head down the stairs and turn left to walk along the footpath. Cross Erina St and turn left into William St Mall. At the other end of the mall, head diagonally through Kibble Park and cross Henry Parry Drive at the lights. Walk uphill along Donnison Street – when the street bends right, continue instead straight up the hill into Rumbalara Environmental Education Centre car park. The 'EEC' provides environmental education and fieldwork opportunities to students, teachers and the wider Central Coast community.

## Walk directions

1 From the car park, follow the *Rumbalara Environmental Education Centre* arrow along the footpath to the track head at the back of the buildings, signposted *Walking Trail*.

2 Head up the steps and along the track and after crossing a small wooden bridge, turn right at an intersection with a management trail. Further up the hill, you will come to another intersection at the bottom of a metal staircase, signposted *Casuarina Track*.

3 Follow the *Picnic Areas* arrow up the staircase, then head along the sandstone path and steps to an intersection marked by a track information board and a *Casuarina Track* sign.

4 Turn right and walk down the hill, towards the gate. After passing a *Rumbalara Reserve* signpost, walk around the gate to the middle of the parking area near John Whiteway Drive.

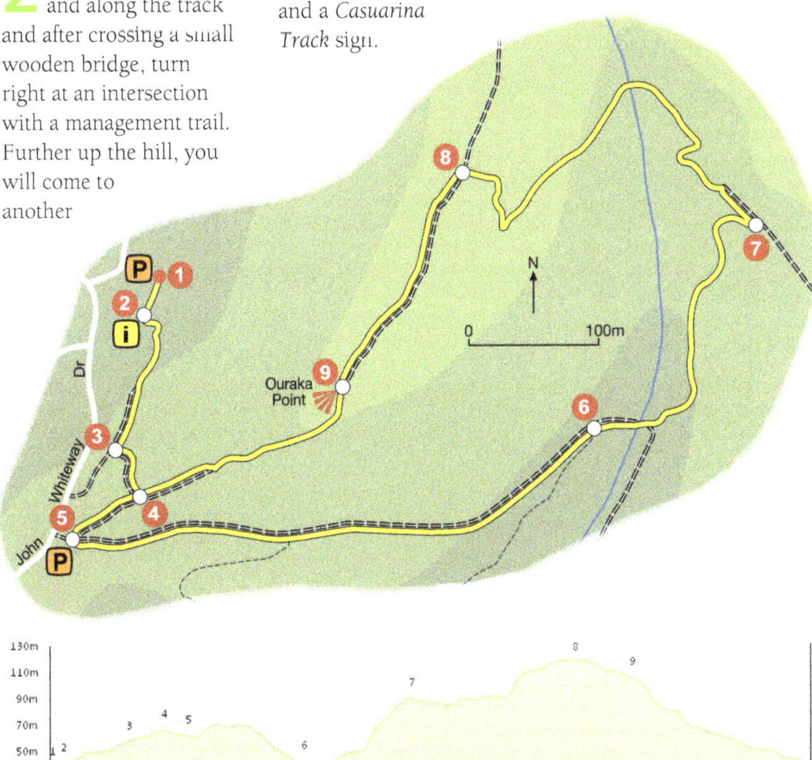

**5** Turn left and follow the management trail away from the road and around a gate. Follow the *White St* arrow along the management trail as it winds around the hill, descending gently through the forest to an intersection beside an *Interpretative Centre* arrow pointing back the way you came.

**6** Continue straight ahead, keeping the old quarry site to the right. After passing a *Cappers Gully* signpost, follow the *Ouraka Point* arrow up the steps, crossing some short metal footbridges before climbing more steeply through the forest. A lot of sandstone steps (and some metal stairs) will follow, before you meet with an intersection, with a *Rainforest Track* signpost pointing back to *Cappers Gully*.

**7** Turn left to follow the management trail in the opposite direction to the *Bay View Ave* arrow. After 50 metres turn left, following the *Ouraka Point* arrow down the steps. Walk on through the forest, crossing two short metal footbridges and heading up a long set of steps, arriving at an intersection with another *Rainforest Track* signpost pointing back to *Cappers Gully*.

**8** Turn right, following the *Picnic Areas* arrow for about 30 metres

to see a sculpture of Charles Sturt. Back at the intersection follow the *Ouraka Point* arrow along the management trail. After a short distance you'll pass an informal, unfenced lookout area and, later, a boulder in the middle of the trail with a signpost indicating *Ouraka Point*.

**9** Walk down the paved steps and past some large boulders to some more steps. Keep going across the end of a management trail, down a metal staircase to veer right at the next intersection. Soon you will come back to waypoint 4 – a familiar intersection marked by an information board and a *Casuarina Track* sign. Turn right down the stairs and retrace your original steps to the Rumbalara EEC and car park.

# 7 Ironbark and Flannel Flower circuit

Taking you along two popular walking tracks and visiting some of the great sights in the upper section of the Rumbalara Reserve, this walk heads through forests and lookouts with views across parts of Gosford and the surrounding areas. The reserve is home to a wide range of flora and fauna, ranging from the relatively dry 'Coastal Narrabeen Ironbark Forest' to pockets of temperate rainforest. The area is rich in wildlife and sugar gliders, brush-tailed possums, blue-tongued lizards and tree snakes can be seen if you are patient - and lucky. The Yaruga picnic area is well-equipped and close to nearby lookouts and walking tracks.

## At a glance

**Grade:** Medium

**Time:** 1 hr

**Distance:** 2.1 km circuit

**Ascent/descent:** 110 metres ascent/descent

**Conditions:** All seasons, gates are locked each evening at 2000

**Getting there:**

**Car:** Parking at the Yaruga picnic area in the Rumbalara Reserve, on Dolly Ave, Springfield

**GPS of start/end:** -33.4255, 151.3553

## Walk directions

1 Head from the BBQs past the information board and toward the toilet block. Turn left just before the toilets and follow the *Nurrunga Picnic Area* arrow down the paved steps. The track leads gently downhill before flattening out and winding around the side of the hill. Ignoring tracks to the left and right, follow the main track until you come to an intersection with a management trail with a *Flannel Flower Track* signpost pointing back to the *Yaruga Picnic Area*.

2 Veer left down the hill. Presently you will arrive at an intersection with a paved path, signposted *Casuarina Track*.

3 Turn right, following the *Nurrunga Picnic Area* arrow, climbing gently for about 180 metres before arriving at a track junction with signposts for the *Ironbark Loop*, the *Casuarina Track* and the *Flannel Flower Track*.

4 Follow the *Loop to Gosford* arrow to the left along the *Casuarina Track*. Continue straight through the next intersection, following the *Nurrunga Picnic Area* arrow (*Ironbark Loop* sign), keeping the views of Gosford to the left. Soon you come to another intersection, with another *Ironbark Loop* signpost pointing back *To Casuarina Track*, and a sculpture of Matthew Flinders.

5 Head in the opposite direction to the *To Casuarina Track* arrow and walk across the end of the picnic area to the sculpture of Sir Charles Kingsford Smith.

6 Turn right at the sculpture and walk along the edge of the picnic area in the direction pointed to by Sir Charles' raised right elbow. Follow the *To Casuarina Track* arrow along the trail, past a toilet block to a sign beside

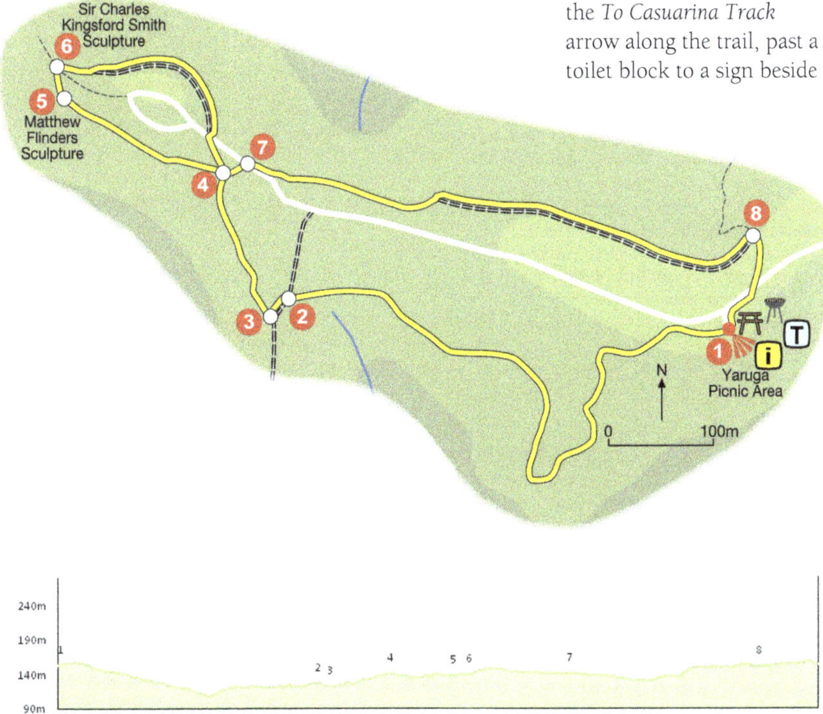

the road pointing back to *Nurrunga Picnic Area*. Cross the road and trek a short distance to to waypoint 4. This time go with the *Loop to Yaruga Picnic Area* arrow, head between the metal posts and across the edge of the small car park, then cross the road to a *Flannel Flower Track* signpost pointing back to *Yaruga Picnic Area*.

Nurrunga Picnic Area

**7** Head along the Loop to *Yaruga Picnic Area* track and down the hill for a short distance before passing under some power lines. Veer right to follow the management trail up the hill and continue past a pipe access point on your left. After a while you reach a 'T' intersection with tracks on the left and right (a water reservoir is visible straight ahead).

**8** Turn right and take the bush track up the steps to the road. Veer right here and follow the road gently up the hill towards the sandstone walls of the nearby Yaruga picnic area.

Sculpture of Matthew Flinders

## Central Coast culture - sculptures in Rumbalara

There are four bronze sculptures in the Rumbalara Reserve that were commissioned as a "Salute to Famous Australians": Captain Charles Sturt, Edward Eyre, Sir Charles Kingsford Smith and Matthew Flinders. They were commissioned for the State Bicentennial Celebrations of 1987. Smith and Flinders, at the Nurrunga picnic area, are the most easily seen.

# 8 Rainforest walk to Nurrunga picnic area

This is an extended version of the Rumbalara Reserve Rainforest Walk. After walking through some beautiful pockets of rainforest, you move to the upper section of the reserve, enjoying views across Gosford and the surrounding areas. Parts of the track are quite steep, although the well-formed tracks - with plenty of steps - make the walking a bit easier. This walk also takes you past three of the four Rumbalara bronze sculptures.

## At a glance

**Grade:** Medium

**Time:** 1 hr

**Distance:** 2.2 km one way

**Ascent/descent:** 200 metres ascent/50 metres descent

**Conditions:** All seasons

**Getting there:**

**Train:** From Gosford station, walk south along Mann St, left onto Georgiana Terrace and right onto Henry Parry Dr to the track head just past the 2GO building, opposite Frederick St

**Bus:** 22 (Red Bus Line) from Gosford station (about every hour) to York St near White St - walk back to Frederick St and turn right to follow it north, crossing Henry Parry Dr to come to the start of the walk

**Car:** Plenty of free parking in Frederick St near Henry Parry Dr - at the end walk back to your car or organise a lift from Nurrunga picnic area; note the entrance gate on Dolly Ave is locked each evening at 2000

**GPS of start:** -33.4338, 151.3469

**GPS of end:** -33.4231, 151.349

## Walk directions

**1** From the track head at Frederick Street and Henry Parry Drive, follow the *Cappers Gully* arrow on the *Rainforest Track* sign along the bush track away from the road. After about 140 metres, the track bends to the left at an arrow post and crosses a small gully, coming to an intersection with a management trail.

**2** Follow the trail to the right. Presently you will pass a plaque marking the handover of Cappers Gully Reserve; continue, bending to the left to the bottom of a metal staircase. Climb up to an intersection with a *Rainforest Track* signpost pointing back to *Henry Parry Drive*.

Statue of Charles Sturt

# 8 Rainforest walk to Nurrunga picnic area

3 Turn right through the vines and ferns, crossing a small metal bridge and continuing past a couple of old picnic tables. You will come to a *Rainforest Track* signpost pointing back to *Henry Parry Drive*. Next to the intersection is an old, fenced square-cut quarry beside Cappers Gully.

4 Turn right and follow the management trail in the opposite direction to the *Interpretive Centre* arrow, keeping the fenced area to the right. Veer left at the *Cappers Gully* signpost, following the *Ouraka Point* arrow up the steps and along the track. Cross some short metal footbridges and head up more steeply through the forest. After a

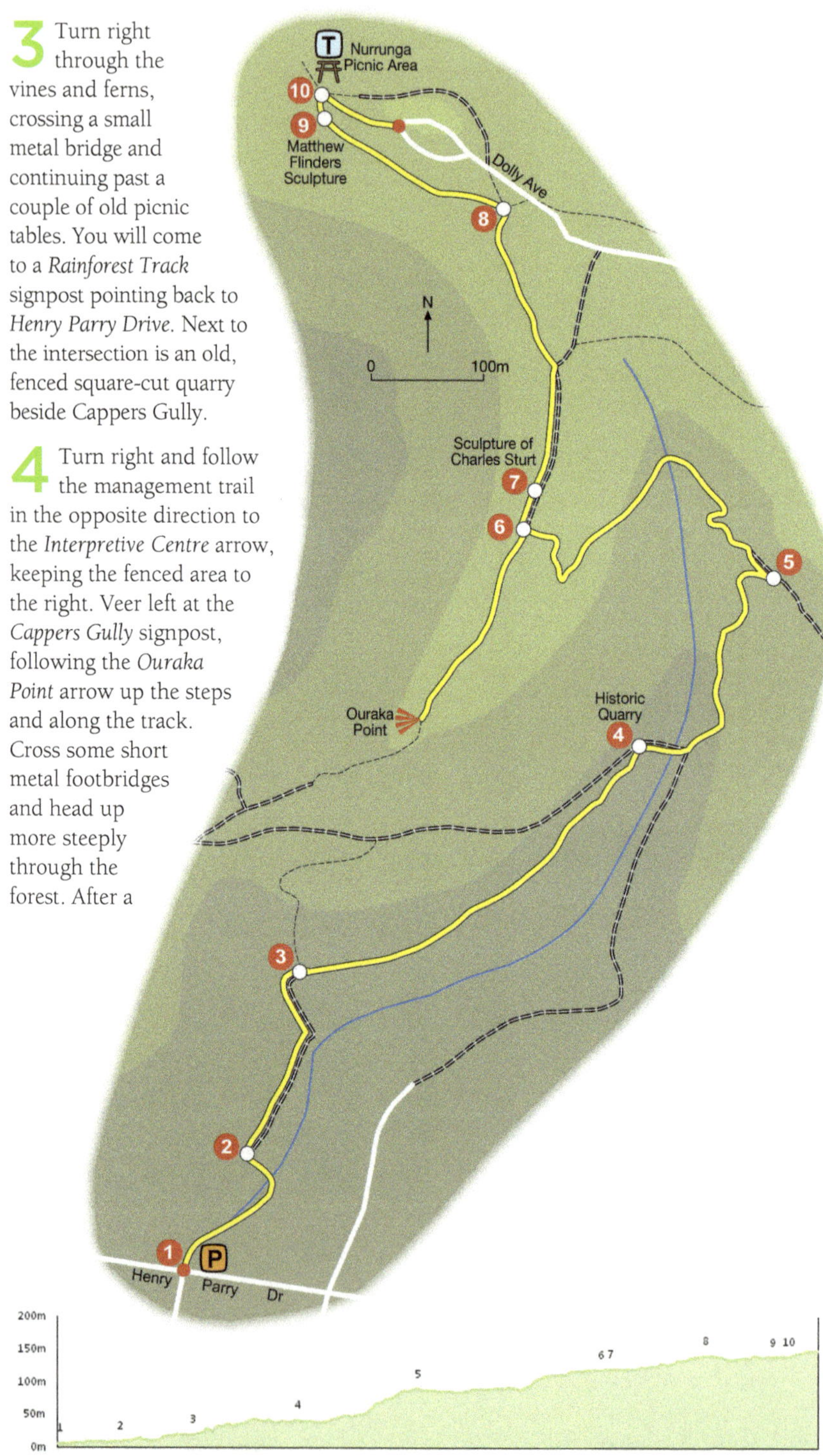

lot of sandstone steps and some sets of metal stairs you will eventually come to an intersection with a *Rainforest Track* signpost pointing back to *Cappers Gully*.

**5** Follow the management trail to the left until you come to another intersection. Turn left with the *Ouraka Point* arrow and head down the steps, meandering for some time through the forest, crossing two short metal footbridges and climbing a long set of sandstone steps followed by a metal staircase. This brings you to an intersection with a management trail and another *Rainforest Track* sign pointing back to *Cappers Gully*.

**6** Follow the *Ouraka Point* arrow downhill to the left and through the forest to find the Ouraka Point lookout and some views over Gosford and Brisbane Water. Retrace your steps to the main track and follow the *Picnic Areas* arrow along the management trail for about 30 metres to the sculpture of Charles Sturt, an early Australian explorer.

**7** About 100 metres or so further, turn left, following the *Nurrunga Picnic Area* arrow along the paved track. After about 170 metres of gentle climbing you will come to a four-way track junction signposted with the *Ironbark Loop*, the *Casuarina Track* and the *Flannel Flower Track*.

**8** Turn left, following the *Loop to Gosford* arrow along the *Casuarina Track* for about 70 metres. Continue through the intersection, following the *Nurrunga Picnic Area* arrow along the *Ironbark Loop*. After about 100 metres you will come across the sculpture of Matthew Flinders, the navigator and cartographer.

**9** Continue in the opposite direction to the *To Casuarina Track* arrow, crossing the end of the picnic area to the sculpture of Sir Charles Kingsford Smith, the well known aviator, who made the first trans-Pacific flight from the United States to Australia.

**10** Turn right and walk across the middle of the picnic area towards the tower, then head up a rocky track and steps, past a *Nurrunga Picnic Area* sign, to find the end of Dolly Avenue.

# 9 Gosford to Lisarow

This is a great way to explore the ridge-top bushland between Gosford and Lisarow. Passing through Rumbalara and Katandra Reserves, there are several picnic areas, lookouts and other facilities scattered along the way. At times you will forget you are anywhere near houses while at others you will be enjoying vistas of the Central Coast. Much of the road walk toward the end is through a rural setting.

## At a glance

**Grade:** Medium

**Time:** 4 hrs 30 mins

**Distance:** 11.3 km one way

**Ascent/descent:** 480 metres ascent/460 metres descent

**Conditions:** Best to avoid hot days

**Getting there:**

**Train:** Frequent rail services between Gosford and Lisarow

**Bus:** Frequent but services between Gosford and Lisarow

**Car:** Drive to the Rumbalara EEC at the end of Donnison St, Gosford, and start just before waypoint 2

**GPS of start:** -33.4235, 151.3418

**GPS of end:** -33.3822, 151.3702

St John Lookout

## Walk directions

**1** From Gosford train station head out the main eastern exit and cross the Pacific Highway using the glass-covered footbridge. On the other side of the bridge, head down the stairs and turn left to walk along the footpath. Cross Erina St and turn left into William St Mall. At the other end of the mall, head diagonally through Kibble Park and cross Henry Parry Drive at the lights. Walk uphill along Donnison Street – when the street bends right, continue instead straight up the hill into Rumbalara Environmental Education Centre car park. The 'EEC' provides environmental education and fieldwork opportunities to students, teachers and the wider Central Coast community. From the car park, follow the *Rumbalara Environmental Education Centre* arrow along the footpath to the track head at the back of the buildings, signposted *Walking Trail*.

**2** Turn left, following the *Walking Trail* arrow up the steps and along the track to cross a small wooden bridge. Turn right at the intersection and follow the management trail gently up the hill before you reach an intersection at the bottom of a metal staircase, signposted *Casuarina Track*.

**3** Follow the *Picnic Areas* arrow left up the staircase. Continue to the intersection with a management trail, turning left to follow the *Picnic Areas* arrow up the hill. When you come to the base of some steps (with a metal staircase to the left), head up these steps and across the end of the management trail, up the long flight of sandstone steps and past some large boulders to the signposted *Ouraka Point*. There are views over Gosford and the surrounding areas and Brisbane Water from here.

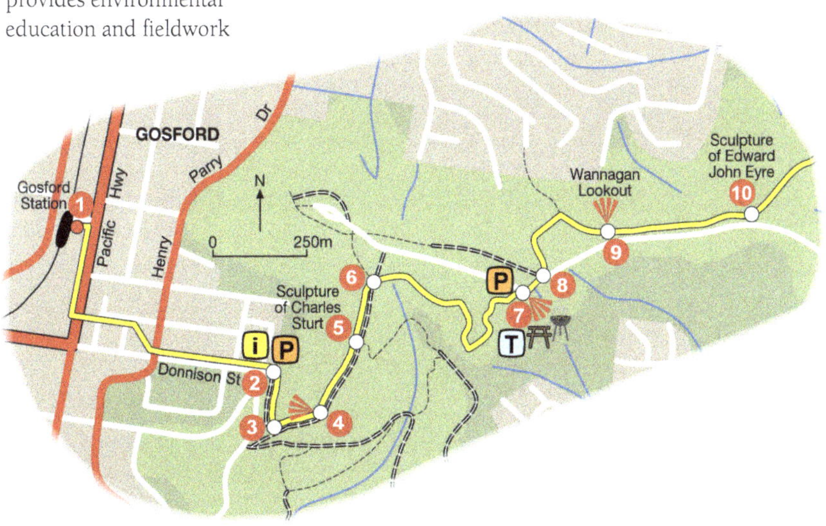


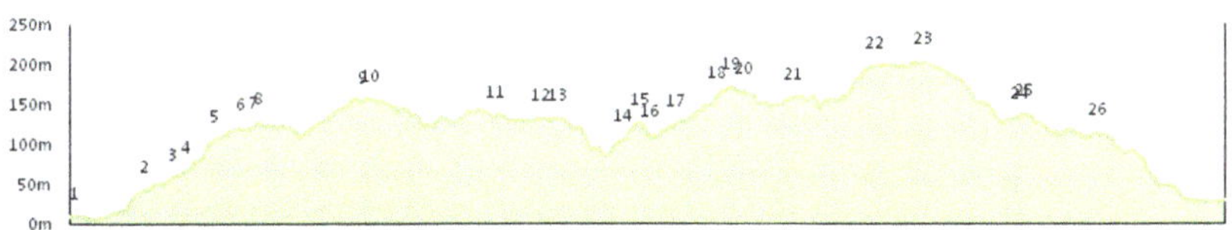

# 9 Gosford to Lisarow

4 Take the management trail up the hill to pass some more filtered views over Gosford. Head straight through the intersection, following the *Picnic Areas* arrow along the management trail. After about 30 metres, you will reach a sculpture of Charles Sturt.

5 Keep the views of Gosford to the left, walking for another 140 metres before coming to an intersection signposted *Casuarina Track*. Veer right and in 30 metres you will come to another intersection with a bush track and a *Flannel Flower Track* sign.

6 Turn right and follow the *Yaruga Picnic Area* arrow down the hill. Keep walking past occasional sandstone steps and through an intersection with a bush track on the left, and another soon after on the right. Continue up the steps to find a clearing and the toilet block at Yaruga Picnic Area. Turn right and follow the paved path past the information board to the BBQs. There are a couple of lookout points at the edge of the picnic area with views out across Gosford and the surrounding areas. The short walk across to Yaruga Lookout from the BBQs is worth the effort.

7 Walk across the picnic area towards the road, then down the steps, veering right and following the road gently down the hill to an intersection with a track, beside a low boulder, on the left (about 100 metres ahead of the nearby reservoir).

8 Take the left-hand track around the low boulder, keeping the reservoir to your right. Head straight through the next intersection, following the track down the steps. Veer left at a rock outcrop and wind down the hill before levelling out and passing an intersection with a faint track to the left. Keep to the right, heading gently up the hill and bending to the right, winding through some

rocky scenery before reaching the Wannagan Lookout, with views to the north from the top of the rocky cliff.

9 Continue up the hill away from the lookout, ignoring the track to the right and taking the left-hand track along the side of the hill. Upon reaching an intersection with a management trail turn left and head towards the sculpture of Edward John Eyre, one of Australia's most famous explorers.

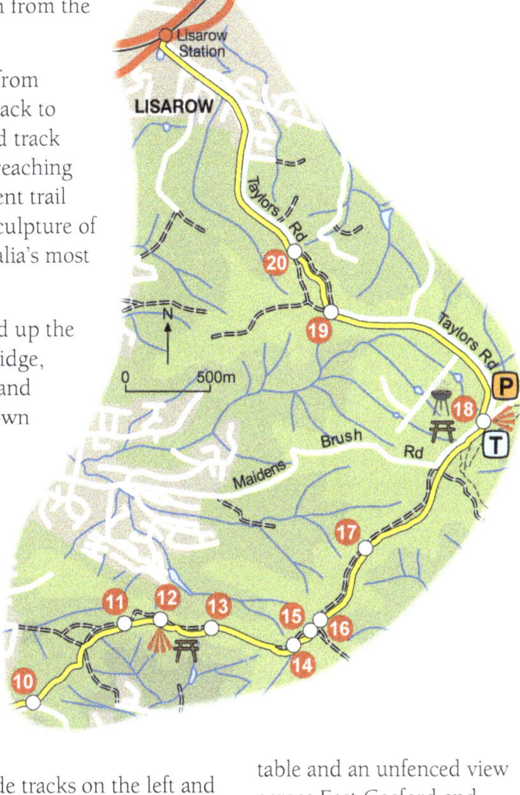


10 Pass the statue and head up the track to the top of the ridge, past some filtered district views and along a fence before climbing down some steps and through a rocky outcrop to a wide trail. Turn right towards a clearing and intersection under the power lines. Continue straight along the management trail where, ignoring the trails on the left, you will soon come to an intersection with Bradys Gully trail running steeply down to the left. Keep climbing straight up the hill until you reach a clearing and a 'Y' intersection just below a rocky outcrop.

11 Veer right to follow the faint track up the hill, ignoring a few side tracks on the left and continuing up the steps through a cleft in the rock. Follow an arrow post around to the right and across the top of the hill, where you will find a picnic table and an unfenced view across East Gosford and Brisbane Water.

12 The track will lead you through another rocky outcrop and down the hill to an intersection with a management trail. Veer right across the saddle and up the hill to another intersection, just before a locked gate. Turn right and head up the steps through the rocks, following the fence for a short time to find another picnic table and an unfenced view across Springfield, East Gosford and Brisbane Water.

**13** Continue along the fence and past a locked gate and bench seat (with a view to the right), then veer left towards another locked gate and a management trail. Follow the wide trail uphill to veer right at a 'Y' intersection marked with two timber posts.

**14** Follow the sign up the narrower track and steps, coming to the top of the hill and the disused Erina Trig station. This station was part of a national geodetic survey established during the 1970's and the view is limited due to overgrowth of trees. You are now at the halfway point!

**15** Continue down the hill and some stairs to find a management trail next to a pond.

**16** Head right towards the power lines, turning left along a fence to a three-way intersection with the Clyde Road management trail. Continue straight, passing the locked gate and fence for the private residence on the left. After about 480 metres turn right at an intersection with the Mouat Trail and an arrow post on the right.

**17** Walk up the steps along the horse track, passing over a rocky outcrop (beware of the cliff drop on the right) before the track bends right, leaving the view to Toomeys management trail behind. You'll trek past some large boulders and through the bush before heading up some steps and passing some informal tracks at a small rock platform. Soon the track leads to a four-way intersection, with *Graves Walk* management trail and a locked gate up the trail to the left. Continue straight past the post with a lilac strip, winding through the bush to a three-way intersection, with a sign pointing back *To Rumbalara Reserve*. Keep walking straight up the hill, where you will eventually reach a large clearing. Walk across the clearing towards the picnic area, to the car park and information sign.

St John picnic area

**18** A side trip to St John lookout is possible here, heading past the BBQ shelters and toilet block to the viewpoint, now upgraded to provide a safer platform and easier access, as well as views overland and out to the ocean. (Please take extra care not to drop anything from the platform as the Guringai Walk passes below.) Back at the main track, turn up the driveway and right onto Toomeys Road. Keep on the main road as it become Taylors Road and bends left. About 400 metres after passing Tapley Road you will come to a dirt clearing and locked gate at the end of Taylors Road (south).

**19** Head around the locked gate and up the dirt management trail. A few metres after the end of the fence turn right down the link track (ignoring another track on the right) and onto a wide management trail. Turn left and walk along the management trail, which leads you around the hill and a locked gate to Taylors Road (north).

20 Take the dirt road to the right. After about 650 metres, the road becomes sealed and passes Beray Close. Keep left at the following 'T' intersection, taking Taylors Road past the school (where the road becomes Chamberlain Road). Presently you will reach a 'T' intersection with the *Pacific Highway*. Cross at the lights and turn right, following the footpath up the ramp to Lisarow Station.

## Edward John Eyre

Eyre was one of Australia's most famous explorers, awarded the founder's gold medal from the Royal Geographical Society in 1847. Previously, in 1841, he was appointed as local resident magistrate and protector of Aborigines. He summed up his work like this:

*"Moorundie was a District densely populated by Natives and in which prior to 1841 no settler had ventured to locate, and where (before I was stationed there) frightful scenes of bloodshed, rapine and hostility between the Natives and Parties coming overland with Stock had been of very frequent occurrence, but where, from the time of my arrival, and up to the date of my leaving not a single case of serious injury or aggression ever took place on the part of the Natives against the Europeans, whilst the district became rapidly and extensively occupied by Settlers and by Stock".*

Eyre also served as lieutenant-governor for New Zealand, lieutenant-governor for St Vincent (West Indies), governor for Leeward Islands, governor for Antigua and governor-in-chief for Jamaica.

# 10 Katandra Reserve Explorer

This walk offers a great way to explore the many highlights of Katandra Reserve. Starting at the lower picnic area, you circumnavigate Seymour Pond via the Waterman Walk, winding through some interesting Strangler Fig trees in the rainforest. As the walk climbs higher, the forest dries out a little, which opens up more views. Taking the Guringai walk along the base of the cliff will then bring you up to St John picnic area and lookout. After enjoying the views from the top, you'll take Graves walk down along the ridge and back to your starting point.

## At a glance

**Grade:** Medium

**Time:** 2 hrs 45 mins

**Distance:** 5.3 km circuit

**Ascent/descent:** 350 metres ascent/descent

**Conditions:** All seasons

**Getting there:**

**Bus:** Catch the 22 or 23 (Red Bus Service) from Gosford Station to The Entrance Rd, then walk up Carlton Rd and right onto Milina Rd, left onto Wattle Tree Rd then left onto Katandra Rd, following this to the end (about a 2km walk)

**Car:** Drive to the intersection of Katandra Rd and Croton Ave, Holgate - there is a car park up the driveway mentioned at waypoint 2

**GPS of start/end:** -33.415, 151.3965

## Walk directions

1 From the gate, walk (or drive) up the sealed driveway to the car park and picnic area. The basic picnic area is in front of the ranger's residence and is open from 0700-1800 daily. You will find toilets, two picnic tables and an information sign.

2 At the top of the car park, turn right and follow the *Seymour Pond* and *Waterman Walk* signs along the clear track. Head down a series of steps and, shortly after turning right at a locked gate you will come to a three-way intersection marked with two blue/white arrows on a post. Follow the arrow downhill to the

Inside a strangler fig

left and into a palm-filled valley. Upon passing the *Commemorating 10 years of bushcaring in Katandra Reserve* plaque, the track bends right and around a sharp left-hand bend and the number 5 post (and old wombat hole). Trek around the gully, crossing a few small bridges to find another picnic area and *Seymour Pond*. The pond is fed by a spring from the cliffs at the reserve top, and is home to waterbirds, large lizards and other wildlife. Note, swimming is not allowed. Seymour Pond Picnic Area is on the dam wall and has a couple of picnic tables.

**3** Turn left, keeping the pond close by on the right. Presently the trail will lead you to a viewing platform with long bench seats - informally named Waterman view.

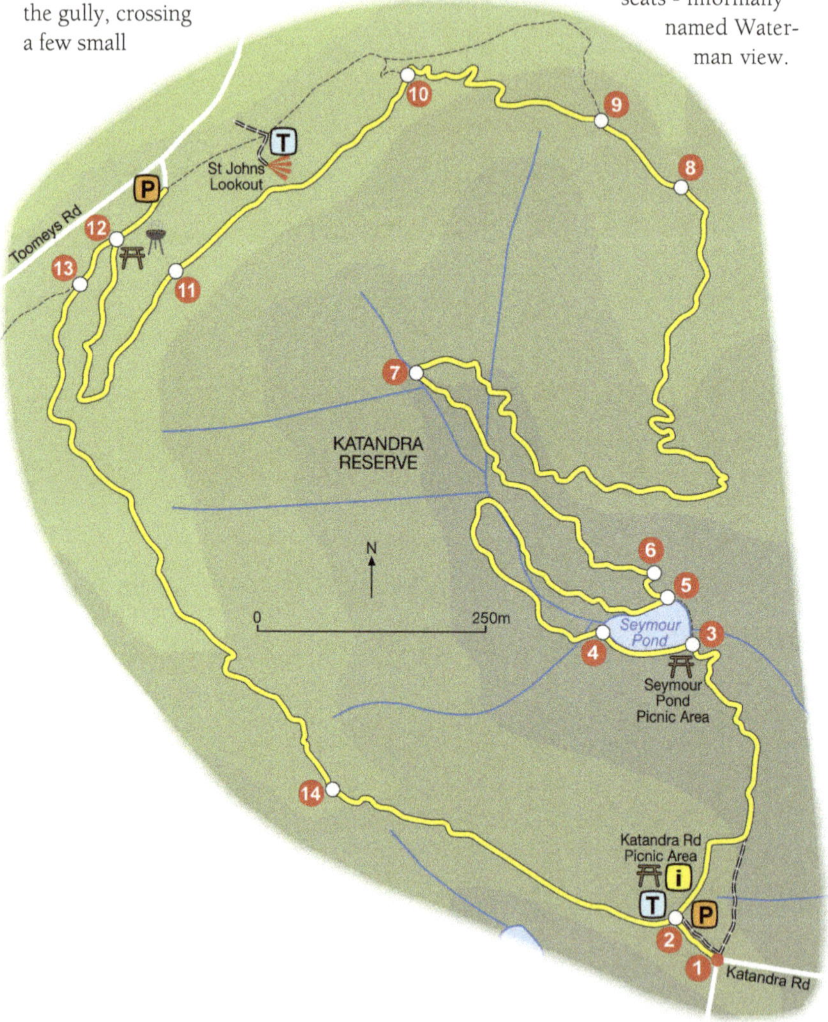

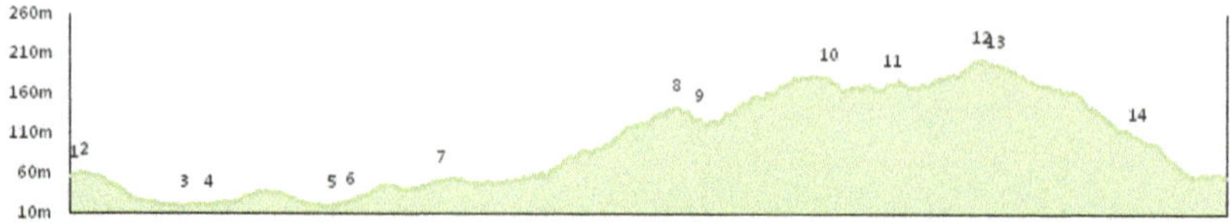

This is a good vantage point to enjoy the water birds and lizards in the area.

4 Take the timber track to the left, crossing over a few small bridges and across a bigger bridge, just after a bench seat. After crossing a few more small bridges you will come to a three-way intersection on a timber board walk at the other side of the pond.

5 Follow the *Toomey Walk* sign to the left. The walk leads you along the gully and up the timber steps as they bend right, bringing you to the number 4 post, next to the Strangler Fig 'tube'. The scientific name of the tree is *ficus obliqua* and it is listed on the Significant Tree Register. This small-leaved fig has grown around a large fallen log which has long-since rotted away, leaving a knotted tubular structure.

6 At the top of the steps turn left around the Fig. After crossing a small creek, head up a long flight of timber stairs, coming eventually to post 3, a large Turpentine Tree. Crossing a few more creeks, head along the valley floor to a large timber platform and an even larger Strangler Fig with a fascinating root structure. The platform is shaded and the bench seat makes an inviting place to sit and soak up the surroundings.

7 Head up the stairs to the right and along the track through the valley. After crossing a few creeks you soon leave the dense forest and start to climb the hill. A couple of longer sets of stairs will help with the steepness before leading you to a large clearing with a *Toomey walk* sign, marking the end of the *Ridgeway Road* trail.

**8** Take the clear track straight ahead for about 120 metres to a three-way intersection marked with some arrows and timber posts on the left.

**9** Turn left through the timber posts where after about 100 metres you'll pass some interesting rock formations before climbing up the hill. Passing between a cleft in the rock, head up some stairs to a signposted three-way intersection.

**10** Take the *Guringai Walk* down the hill and stairs to the left, walking along the base of the cliff and past a short section littered with broken glass (this is directly below St John Lookout). The track dips down, then up some stairs, coming very close to the base of the cliff and passing a long section of handrail, after which it reaches post 8 next to a large Blackbutt tree. The tree has a brown fibrous bark on the lower half then a smooth grey bark at the top.

**11** Continue up the stairs, along the base of the cliff until you cross a small bridge where the track starts to zigzag up the hill past some large angophoras and grass trees. Soon you come to a large clearing; turn right towards the picnic area, past the car

park and BBQ shelters to a sandstone footpath in front of the toilet block. Follow the footpath to the fenced and signposted *St John Lookout*.

**12** Turning left away from the main picnic area, double back on yourself, and walk towards the *Mount Mouat Walk* and *Graves Walk* signs, where you should turn left again along the track towards the signposted intersection with *Graves Walk* on the left.

**13** Take *Graves Walk*, between the timber posts and down the hill. Pass between a few more timber posts and arrow markers, ignoring the short link track leading to the horse trail on the right. Continue gently downhill (keeping the horse track through the bush to the right), along the ridge and past the number 6 post (there are Aboriginal markings in the stone here). As the ridge narrows to a rocky outcrop, head down the stairs to a large five-way intersection and a locked gate, behind the ranger's residence.

**14** Veer right, following an arrow past the post with the purple strip and down a few sets of steps. Passing a steep trail on the right (leading to Murina Close) keep moving down the hill and a series of steps to where the track flattens out again. Eventually you will be led back to the picnic area and car park at waypoint 2. Turn right to follow the driveway back to the junction of Katandra Road and Croton Avenue.

# 11 Kincumber to Terrigal (via Glasson's Trail)

Exploring the main highlights of Kincumber Mountain Regional Reserve, this walk starts by following Glasson's Trail through a variety of forest cover to Honeman's Rock and picnic area. You will then visit a large cave on Kanning Walk and continue to the views from Colin Watters Lookout. The track then leads down the ridge through some interesting rocky outcrops on the way to Sandringham Close, Terrigal.

### At a glance

**Grade:** Medium

**Time:** 2 hrs

**Distance:** 4.5 km one way

**Ascent/descent:** 220 metres ascent/descent

**Conditions:** Any time

**Getting there:**

**Bus:** Catch the 60, 65 or 66 Busway bus from Gosford station to Kincumber shops (there are usually a couple buses every few hours)

**Car:** Car park at the end of Kincumber St

**GPS of start:** -33.4637, 151.3792

**GPS of end:** -33.4447, 151.4068

## Finding the track

From Kincumber shops (Avoca Drive), head along Bunboona Road from the roundabout, turning left to follow Kincumber Street past the Kincumber Mountain sign. You will find a car park and the start of this walk on the left, just before the large water tank.

## Walk directions

1 Walk to the back of the car park, through the gap in the fence and turn right. Keep the water tank up the hill to the right and head up some timber steps through the rocks and past the back of the tank, coming to a 'T' intersection with a management trail. Turn left and downhill. Around 300 metres on, on a wide sweeping right-hand bend, you'll find a rocky outcrop with a view into the valley on the left. Continue around the bend and up the hill, through a lush section of forest. As you begin to climb again, the trail widens and you will come to a locked gate, road and *Glasson's trail* sign. Cross the road to a small clearing.

2 Walk up the ramp behind the clearing, keeping the road to the left. Head up the steps, between the timber posts and turn right to head up some more steps. The rocky track flattens out somewhat and heads along the top of the ridge among the grass trees before leading you down again to turn right onto the road, then left onto another track after about 10 metres. Walk through the bush for about 100 metres to a picnic shelter, car park and a *Glasson's Trail - Island View Entrance 1300 metres* sign pointing back the way you came.

3 Walk uphill across the car park, following the *Glasson's Trail - Honemans Rock picnic area* sign up the stone steps and to a large clearing. Walk across the grassy area, tending right, then around the Honeman's Rock and up to the mud brick building (available for hire) at the top of the picnic area. The rock was named after Cecil Lyle Honeman, a lease holder on the mountain in 1962.

4 Walk to the car park on the right, then turn left and head up the road. A short distance up the hill, take the first right and follow the *One Way*

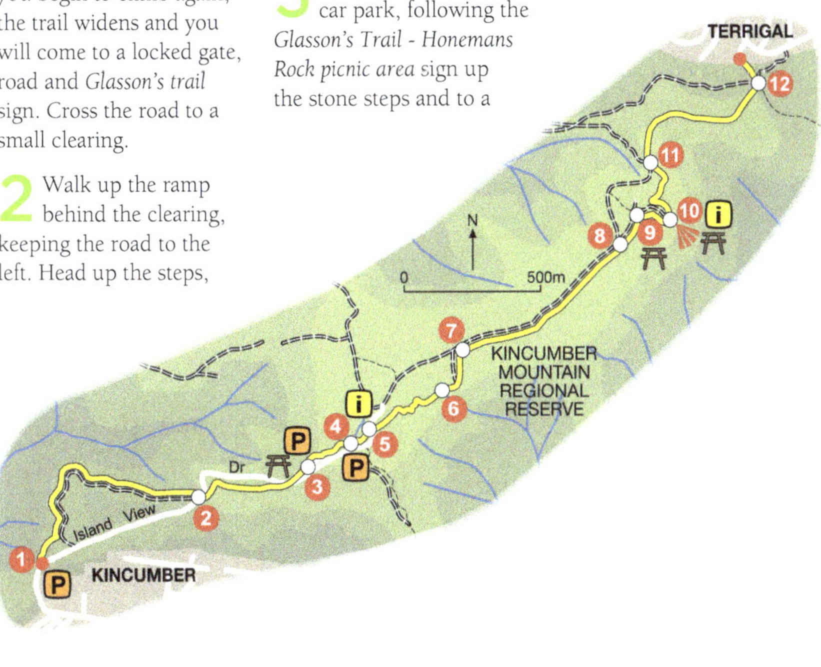

road sign to a locked gate and the *Kanning Walk* sign.

**5** Follow the *Kanning Walk cave 300 metres* sign to the left and around the locked gate. After about 120 metres turn right and follow another *Kanning Walk* sign between two large exposed tree root systems. Soon you will pass along the base of a long rock wall, then down some steel stairs and across a timber bridge, coming to a fairly large sandstone overhang cave with a *cave 100m* sign pointing further along the track. Follow this track for about 150 metres, over a steel platform, up a small rise and down some steel stairs. From the base of these stairs, continue along the flat track to find the unsignposted entrance to the cave between two large boulders on the left. This cave has two main sections. The first is a large cabin, about 7 metres wide and 9 metres deep. There is a small tunnel that extends to a small chamber at the back. The entrance to the cave is behind two large boulders, providing extra shelter. It is believed that this cave was lived in during the early 1930's, cave-living being not uncommon during the depression. It is a great place to rest on hot days.

**6** Veer right, around the base of the rock wall. Soon you pass the *Alternate Return* sign up some steps,

Cave on Kanning Walk

Honeman's Rock

Colin Watters Lookout

eventually heading through a timber barrier to a 'T' intersection with a wide management trail and a few *Kanning Walk* signs.

7 Turn right and follow the *Yanina Walk* sign though the tall wooded forest, passing a few small clearings on the side. You should soon come to a clear and signposted 'Y' intersection with *Colin Watters Lookout* sign.

8 Take the right fork, following the *Colin Watters Lookout* sign uphill for about 80 metres, where you will find a large clearing. Walk through the clearing (passing a shortcut track on the right) and come to an intersection near the far end (just before the picnic table) marked with another *Colin Watters Lookout* sign. The clearing is next to a large communication repeater tower – you will find some natural shade here.

9 Turn right towards *Colin Watters Lookout*, along the narrower management trail, to another intersection. Turn right and walk past the roofed information board (and the other end of the shortcut track) to the lookout which provides a clear view southeast down Picketts Valley to Avoca Lake and Beach.

10 Turn left at the lookout and follow the narrower track, which soon bends left and passes an informal right-hand track to come to a clear intersection with a wider trail back near the large tower. Turn right and follow the track away from the tower, heading past a rocky outcrop and along the flat section to a larger outcrop. Keep the rocks to your left as you walk on between the gum and grass trees, down to a small clearing and intersection with a management trail.

11 Continue downhill to the right, following the top of the ridge. After about 120 metres, take the right fork at a 'Y' intersection and turn right again another 150 metres later, in front of a large dead tree. This track leads you down a few steps and across a flat saddle before turning left down a long series of timber steps, coming to a wide management trail at a 5-way intersection.

12 Turn left, then right, to follow the narrow track between the timber barriers. Head down the track and the concrete steps between two houses, coming to the end of Sandringham Close, Terrigal.

Bullimah Beach Headland

# Bouddi National Park

Bouddi National Park is a beautiful coastal reserve at the mouth of the Hawkesbury River that also extends beyond the land to also protect 300 hectares of marine environment around Maitland Bay. The area is home to several small beaches, campsites, lookouts and some great walks. We have chosen the walks in this chapter to help you discover the main highlights of the park and you will enjoy sweeping ocean vistas, quiet secluded beaches, rocky shorelines, some perched sand dunes and even a shipwreck.

On May 6 1898 during a terrible storm, 24 people lost their lives when the paddle steamer, the S.S. Maitland, smashed against the rocks. After heroic efforts 12 people escaped with their lives and the iron hull can still be seen in Maitland Bay. This park offers an opportunity to explore an environment that will last long after this boat is reclaimed by the sea.

# 12 Box Head Track

Starting on Hawke Head Drive, this walk explores the southernmost ridge in Bouddi NP. The walk provides sweeping views over Woy Woy, Broken Bay, Hawkesbury River and the Tasman Sea. It also takes in views over Lion Island and Pearl Beach from the many rocky outcrops along the Box Head ridge.

## At a glance

**Grade:** Medium

**Time:** 2 hrs

**Distance:** 3.1 kms return

**Ascent/descent:** 130 metres ascent/ descent

**Conditions:** All conditions

**Getting there:**

**Car:** Drive to the car park at the end of Hawke Head Drive, Hardys Bay (off Nukara Ave)

**GPS of start/end:** -33.5343, 151.3471

Tallow Beach Campsite from Hawke Head Drive

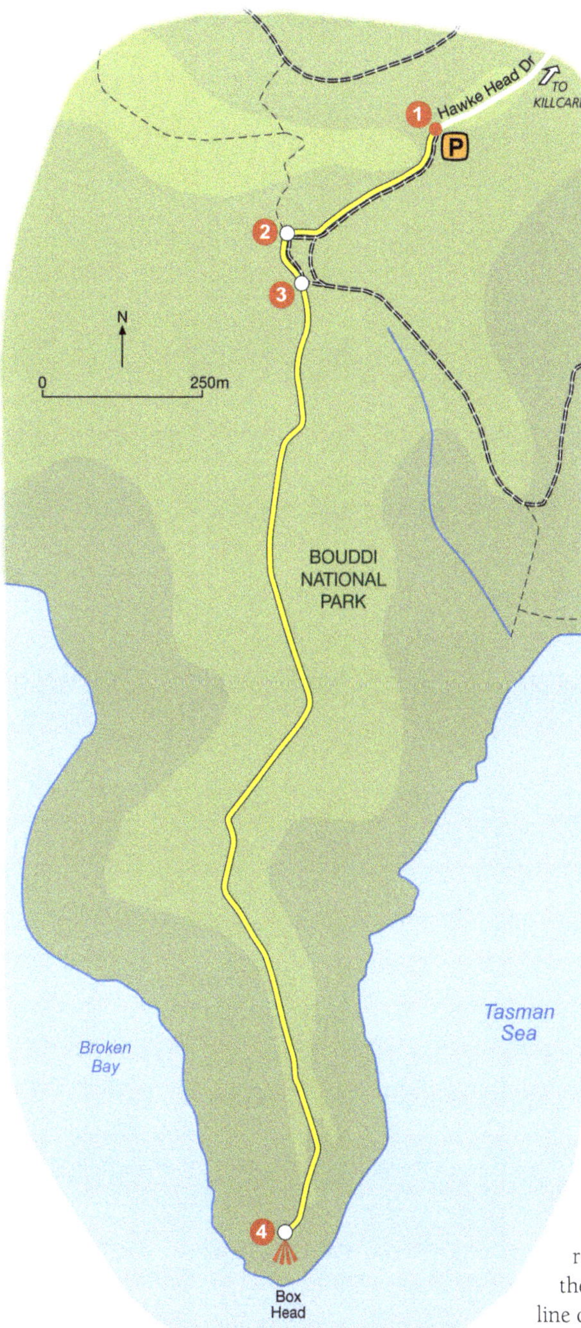


## Walk directions

**1** From the car park, follow the management trail past the *Tallow Beach 900m* signpost. You will soon pass around a gate and continue down the hill, before passing an unfenced cliff warning sign and (ignoring) a Tallow Beach track signpost. Head up the hill to an intersection, signposted with *Tallow and Killcare*.

**2** Turn left, following the *Tallow* arrow along the management trail. After about 60 metres you will come to a signposted intersection for *Box Head* and *Tallow Beach*.

**3** Veer right, following the *Box Head* sign along the track. After a short time, you will cross a rocky area and go through a small clearing. Continue along the track as it narrows and meanders for several hundred metres, crossing more rocky outcrops, then follow the top of the unfenced cliff line of Box Head out to the end of the track at the point itself.

# 12 Box Head Track

4 Box Head is the northern entrance to Broken Bay, and there are panoramic views over the Pacific Ocean, Barrenjoey Head, Lion Island and the rest of the bay. The track to the headland makes it quite accessible, and also has some great views along the way. Note that Box Head is an unfenced area with no facilities. Return the way you came.

Box Head bushtrack

# 13 Bullimah Outlook

Starting from the Maitland Bay Information Centre, this walk heads down and around the hill to follow the spur out to unfenced Bullimah Outlook. The track winds through the bush giving glimpses of Maitland Bay from several rocky landings. The views along the way, and from the lookout are well worth the visit.

## At a glance

**Grade:** Medium

**Time:** 1 hr 15 mins

**Distance:** 2.3 kms return

**Ascent/descent:** 100 metres ascent/descent

**Conditions:** Best views on sunny day

**Getting there:**

**Bus:** Catch Busways route 61 from Gosford Station to the intersection of The Scenic Rd and Maitland Bay Dr; or Catch Busways route 59 from Woy Woy Station to the intersection of Hats Rd and The Scenic Rd, then walk about 1.5 km east along The Scenic Rd to Maitland Bay Dr (infrequent services on weekends, see timetables at www.131500.com.au)

**Car:** Drive to Maitland Bay visitor Centre, on The Scenic Rd, Killcare Heights (near the intersection with Maitland Bay) - there is a car park next to the information centre

**GPS of start/end:** -33.5201, 151.3827

# 13 Bullimah Outlook

## Walk directions

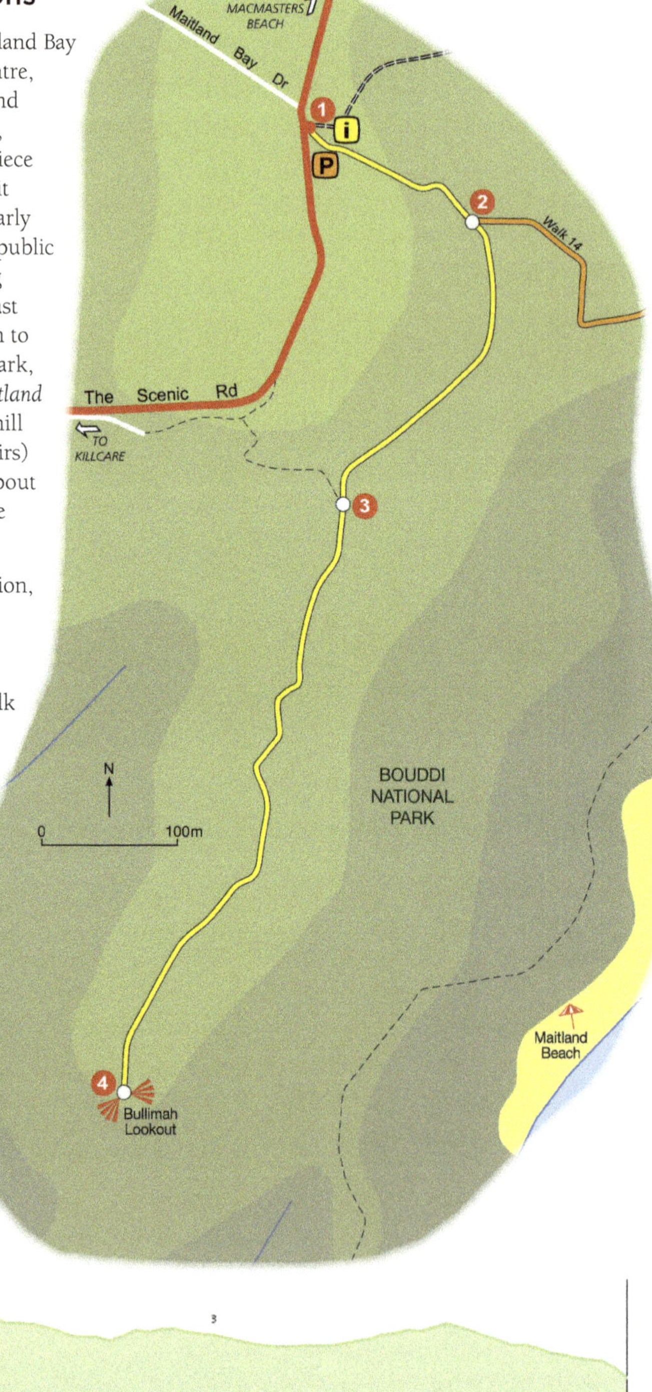


**1** Start at the Maitland Bay Information Centre, once the old Maitland Store and residence, and an influential piece of infrastructure as it acted as a hub for early tourism. There is a public phone and drinking water here. Head past the information sign to the end of the car park, then follow the *Maitland Bay* sign down the hill (including some stairs) to an intersection about 180 metres from the information centre.

**2** At the intersection, turn right and follow the *Bullimah Spur* sign along the narrower track. Walk around the hill then wind through some boulders - soon the track rises and comes to a fainter one on the right, about 350 metres from point 2 (this faint track leads up to Marie Byles Lookout).

3 Continue along the main track towards the sea, winding down the hill and passing a few short side tracks to views on the left. Continue down the ridge to Bullimah Outlook, which is marked by a plaque in the rock.

4 Bullimah Outlook is an unfenced lookout perched on the end of Bullimah Spur, overlooking much of Bouddi National Park and the coastline. The views from the lookout are quite scenic, with the northern beaches, Lion Island and Broken Bay all revealing themselves. The lookout commemorates Charles Darcy Roberts, once a trustee of Bouddi National Park and a bushwalker. Return the way you came.

Putty Beach from Bullimah Outlook

# 13 Bullimah Outlook

From Bullimah Outlook

# 14 Gerrin Point Circuit

This loop walk starts at Marie Byles Lookout, also known as the Killcare Heights Lookout, named after mountaineer, explorer and avid bushwalker Marie Byles, the first advocate of a Bouddi National Park. The walk showcases the wide range of coastal views and scenery of Bouddi National Park. Optional side-trips to a couple of beaches add some variety to the walk.

Maitland Bay and headland

## At a glance

**Grade:** Medium

**Time:** 2 hrs 30 mins

**Distance:** 5.2 km circuit

**Ascent/descent:** 300 metres ascent/descent

**Conditions:** All seasons

**Getting there:**

**Bus:** Catch Busways route 59 from Woy Woy Station to the intersection of Hats Rd and The Scenic Rd, then walk about 1.1 km east along The Scenic Rd to Marie Byles Lookout; or catch Busways route 61 from Gosford Station to the intersection of The Scenic Rd and Maitland Bay Dr and start the walk at point 2 (see timetables at www.131500.com.au)

**Car:** Drive to Marie Byles Lookout car park, on The Scenic Road, Killcare Heights

**GPS of start/end:** -33.5229, 151.3812

# 14 Gerrin Point Circuit

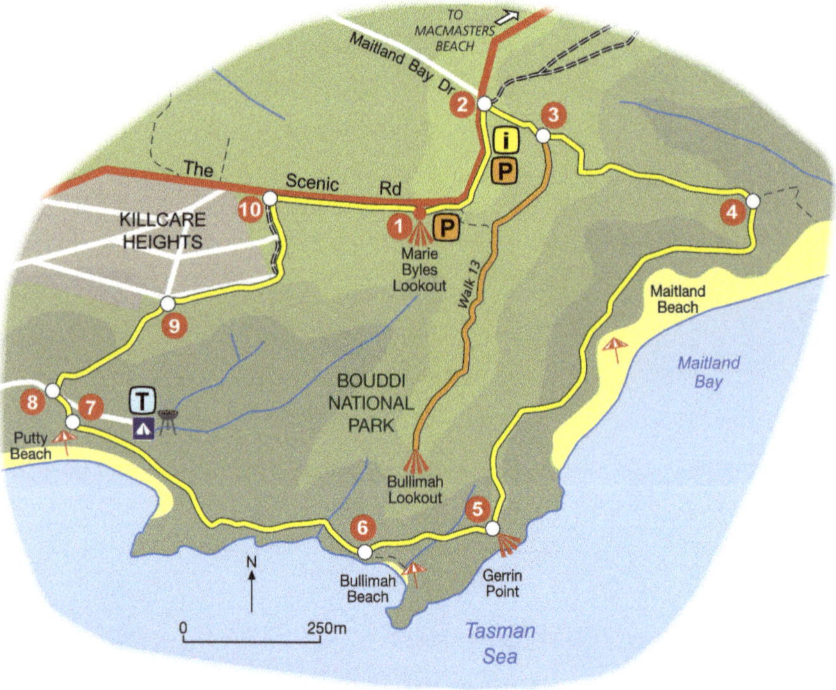

## Walk directions

1 From the car park and lookout, follow the track past the information board, with the water view to the right. After winding through the bush for approximately 25 metres, you will reach an intersection (with a track on the right). Continue straight on, keeping the road above and to the left. Soon the track leads you to the road, which you continue along until, about 200 metres after the large water tank, you come to another car park and the Maitland Bay Information Centre.

Maitland Bay Information Centre and S.S.Maitland Bell

2 At the information centre turn right, passing the information sign to the start of the car park. From the car park, the walk follows the *Maitland Bay* sign down the hill and some stairs to come to an intersection about 180 metres from the information centre.

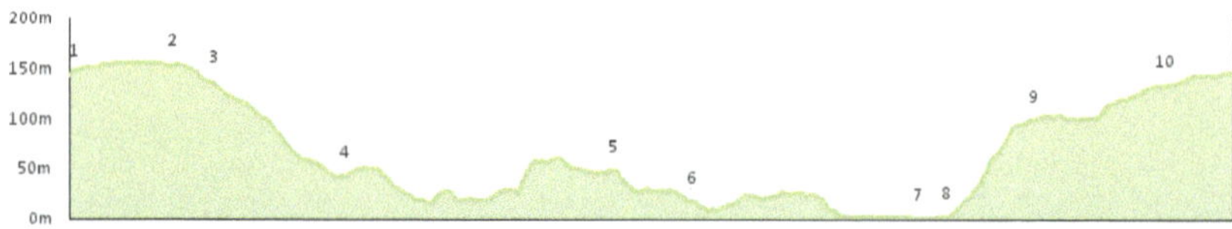

3 Continue straight down the hill following the track down the stairs. You will wind through the forest, passing a rock platform with views over Maitland Bay. Continue down the hill from the platform and after a little while you will cross over a wooden bridge and head down more steps to a signposted intersection.

4 Veer right and walk up the hill, following the track marked by the *Bouddi Coastal Walk* sign. The track goes over many rises and crosses fenced bridges over the valleys between. This continues for about a kilometre, until you arrive in a clearing before a fenced lookout, Gerrin Point.

5 Turn right at this lookout and follow the track down the hill, keeping the water below and to the left. Continue along steps and boardwalks, following the hillside to a signposted intersection.

6 Turn right (turning left takes you down to Bullimah Beach) and walk along the edge of the headland, following the railed pathway. As you round the headland to Putty Beach, you will pass a red rocky area and continue down a staircase onto the beach. Walk approximately 150 metres along the beach, to where the creek has cut through

Stairs from Maitland Bay Information Centre

Gerrin Point rocksheld looking to maitland Bay

the sand. Continue along the beach, keeping the water on the left and after approximately 200 metres, you will reach a spot on the beach opposite a white-roofed building behind the dunes, just before another wide (dry) creek entry.

**7** Turn right here and walk away from the ocean, towards the white-roofed building, then follow the fenced sandy track to Putty Beach camping area.

**8** Cross the road and walk to the far right hand corner of the campsite then follow the track back into the bush. After winding up the hill you come to a fenced house. Turn right here and you will soon come to an intersection with another track. Veer left and after a short distance you will pass a *Bouddi National Park* sign and arrive at Jacqueline Avenue.

**9** Turn right up the avenue then walk past a *No Through Road* sign (on the right) and a line of houses (on the left) and you soon come to the cul-de-sac at the end of the road. From here, walk through the bushes along a track and when this opens up into a management trail, turn left and follow the trail up the hill to an intersection with another management trail (on the left). Go straight ahead and continue up the hill for a short distance. Follow the trail as it narrows and passes between boulders, and continue up the hill to The Scenic Road.

**10** Turn right and walk along the road, with the ocean views to the right, until, after about 350 metres, you'll see on the right the car park you left back at waypoint 1.

## Out and about - Putty Beach Camping Area

Putty Beach camping area is a spacious, grassed area with easy access to the beach. The campsite is also home to many Brush Turkeys. Facilities include drinking water, flush toilets, open-air showers, rubbish bins, BBQ's (gas/electric). Wood fires not permitted. Campsites must be booked in peak periods, up to 3 months in advance. Bookings can be made by phoning (02) 4320 4203. A campsite costs $14/adult (16+) and $7/child (5-15). Park entry and parking: Parking and entry costs $7/24 hours. Single park entry passes can be picked up from Killcare Cellars and General Store - 56 Araluen Drive, Killcare. Alternatively, they can be obtained from ticket dispensers in the picnic and camping areas. General enquiries - call DECCW Central Coast (02) 4320 4200 or 4329 4280.

# 15 Little Beach Trail

This walk from Grahame Drive car park to Little Beach, a 100 metre long stretch of sand and rocks facing out to the Tasman Sea and South Pacific Ocean, follows the management trail straight down the hill through tall forest. Little Beach is popular with surfers, and the campsite provides a nice place for a rest. The campsite has six marked sites, a composting toilet, rubbish bins, gas BBQ and a shelter. A great spot for a BBQ lunch after getting your toes wet.

## At a glance

**Grade:** Easy

**Time:** 30 mins

**Distance:** 1.2 kms return

**Ascent/descent:** 50 metres ascent/descent

**Conditions:** All seasons

**Getting there:**

**Car:** Drive to the car park at the end of Grahame Dr, off The Scenic Rd just north of Bouddi

**GPS of Start:** -33.5098, 151.4123

Grahame Drive Track to Little Beach

Little Beach Camping Area

# 15 Little Beach Trail

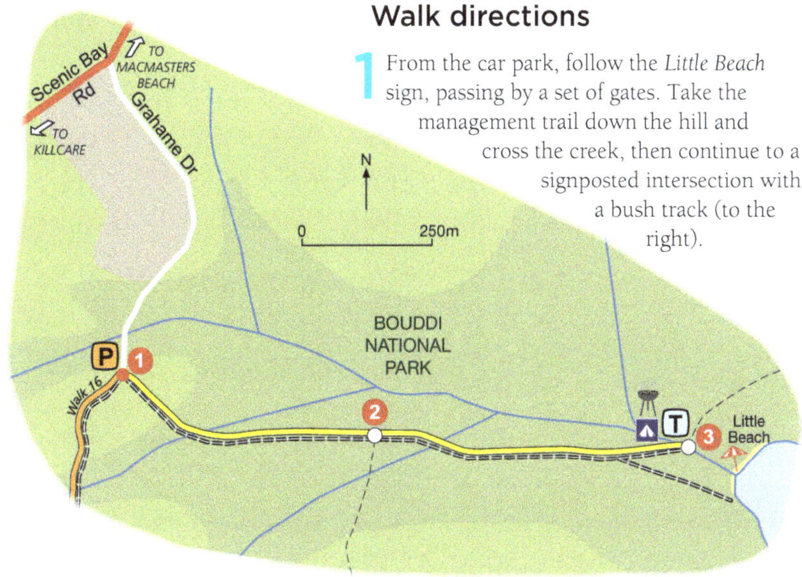


## Walk directions

1 From the car park, follow the *Little Beach* sign, passing by a set of gates. Take the management trail down the hill and cross the creek, then continue to a signposted intersection with a bush track (to the right).

2 Continue along the main trail, following the *Little Beach* sign, for about 300 metres down the hill and you will soon come to the Little Beach campsite and the beach a short distance later.

3 Return the way you came.

Little Beach

# 16 Bouddi Coastal Walk

This is one of the longer walks in the Bouddi National Park and is rich in scenery. The walk follows the coastline, with many side trips to lookouts, beaches and even offers an opportunity to see the wreckage of the S.S. Maitland, which gave its name to Maitland Bay after being wrecked there in 1898. This walk makes a wonderful one-way trip from Graham Drive down to Putty Beach, with views around every corner.

## At a glance

**Grade:** Medium

**Time:** 5 hrs

**Distance:** 8.1 kms one-way

**Ascent/descent:** 370 metres ascent/410 metres descent

**Conditions:** All seasons

**Getting there:**

**Car:** Drive to the car park at the end of Grahame Dr, off The Scenic Rd just north of Bouddi

**Return:** Either arrange a car-shuffle or pick-up prior to starting, or pre-arrange a taxi (Central Coast Taxis, T 131008)

**GPS of start:** -33.5098, 151.4123

**GPS of end:** -33.531, 151.3607

## Walk directions

1 From the car park, follow the *Little Beach* sign along the management trail, passing around a gate. Continue down the hill, cross the creek and climb up the hill out of the gully. You will then wind down to a signposted intersection, with a track to the right.

2 Take this right turn and walk up the hill, following the *Maitland Bay* sign. Head along a white sandy section of track, then continue through the scrub for approximately 300 metres to a signposted intersection in a large sandy clearing.

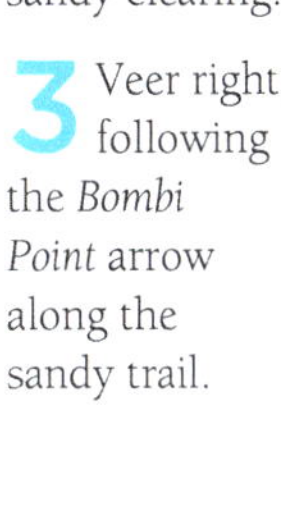

3 Veer right, following the *Bombi Point* arrow along the sandy trail. Follow this as it winds down the hill for some time before climbing to a signposted intersection (*Third Point*, on the left). Turn right and follow the management trail down the hill for about 70 metres to come to a large sandy area marked by a *Little Beach car park* sign (pointing right). From here, follow the management trail left down the hill (in the opposite direction to the *Little Beach car park* sign) then wind down the hill for about 600 metres to come to another larger clearing, with a *Bouddi Coastal Walk* sign.

4 Follow the *Maitland Bay* arrow along the narrower track. Cross the steep Cave Gully (many steps here) then head over a rise to cross a second gully about 350 metres later. After another 300 metres cross a third creek via a wooden bridge, then climb to the top of the stairs and continue along the hillside for about 200 metres to the signposted 'T' intersection.

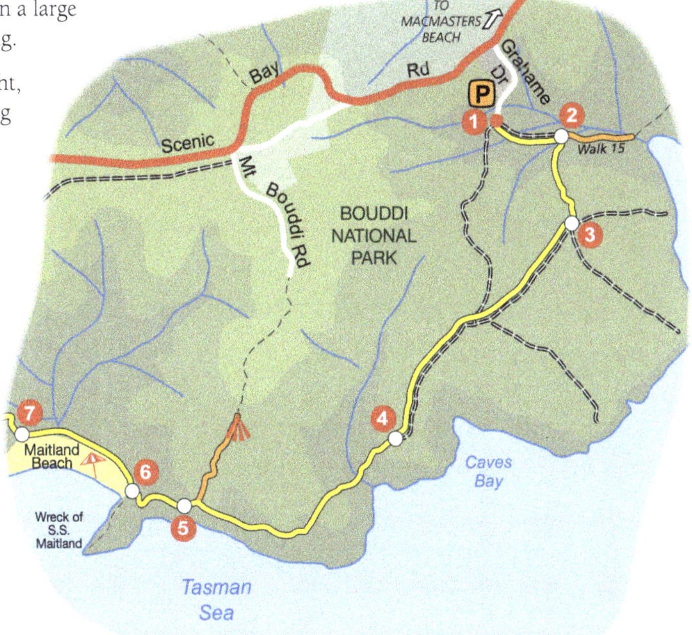


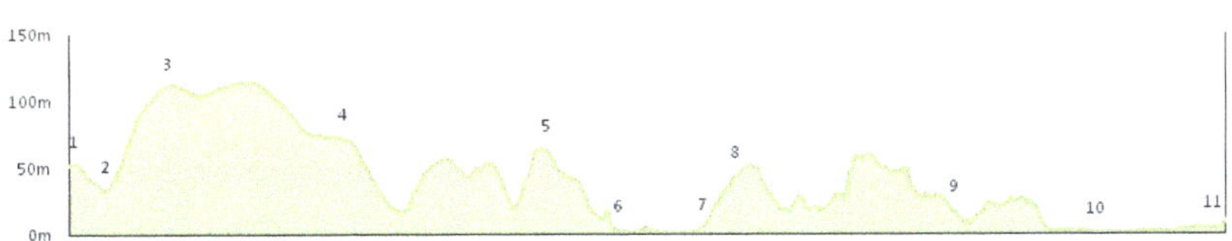

**5** Turn left and follow the *Maitland Bay* arrow along the track. After a while, you will head down into a clearing, on the saddle of the small headland. Follow the track to the right, down some steep steps to the beach.

**6** If you're keen on seeing the Maitland wreck, turn left, and follow the bottom of the cliff line out towards the sea, then continue over rocks and boulders for about 300 metres, to the rock flats at the point. Note that this is not passable at higher tides and during rough seas. To continue on the walk, head back up to waypoint 6, then along the beach for about 600 metres, keeping the ocean to your left. Part way along, a creek often cuts its way through the sand - just before the end of the sand, you will come to the base of some paved steps (leading up away from the beach).

**7** Follow this paved track as it winds up the hill, then straightens out before arriving at a signposted intersection, 250 metres from the beach.

**8** Veer left and walk up the hill, along the track marked by the *Bouddi Coastal Walk* sign. You'll soon return to the coast, with more water views. Continue following the track as it undulates along the cliff top, passing over a few bridges across the valleys, until you come to a clearing and the Gerrin Point lookout. Turn right here and follow the track and boardwalks to a signposted intersection.

**9** Turn right and walk along more boardwalks and a track with a handrail, keeping the water below on the left. After about 500 metres you round the headland and red rocks then follow the steps down onto Putty Beach. From here, walk approximately 350 metres

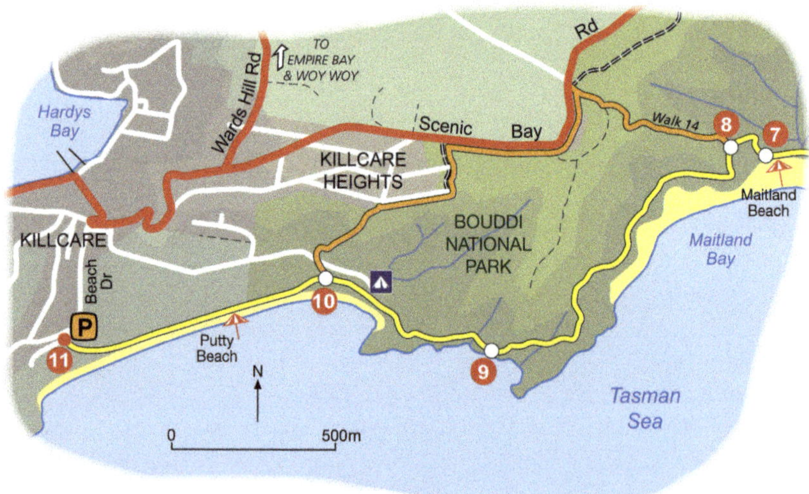


## Walk variation - Bouddi Lookout

From point 5, turn right at the intersection, and follow the *Mt Bouddi* arrow up the hill. Climb the steps to the lookout, at the top of a small rocky hill, 350 metres from point 5. The lookout provides great views of the Bouddi Coast and the Pacific Ocean crashing into the heath-covered headlands in front of the lookout. Retrace your steps back to point 5.

to an access track leading up to a white-roofed building behind the dunes (Putty Beach Camping Area), just before another wide (dry) creek entry.

**10** Continue along the beach for just over a kilometre, keeping the ocean to the left, past many beach access points, until you come to the lifeguard tower (near the car park).

**11** Turn right, leaving the beach, and walk up the hill along a stony path for about 50 metres, to the car park behind the beach.

## Central Coast history - S.S. Maitland Shipwreck

The S.S. Maitland was a paddle steamer brought to Australia from Glasgow, Scotland, to transport people and cargo between the Hunter and the Hawkesbury Rivers. There was no rail line from Newcastle to Sydney in the 1800's. The Maitland was on its route out of the Barrenjoey Headlands when it was overwhelmed by the aptly-named 'Maitland Gale'. The storm which wrecked the Maitland also took numerous other ships on May 6, 1898. Of the 36 passengers aboard the Maitland, 24 lost their lives. Many of the survivors were commended for their heroism. Wreckage of the Maitland can still be seen today, with parts of the boiler and a section of the iron hull strewn across the rock flats of the point. The bay was previously known as Boat Harbour, then renamed Maitland Bay after the disaster in 1898.

Pearl Beach from Mt Ettalong

# Brisbane Water National Park

As the name suggests this park rises out of the Brisbane Water to the west of Gosford. Brisbane Water National Park is traversed by the Great North Walk and features some rugged sandstone environments, waterfalls, lookouts, caves and mangroves. The park provides a wide range of walking opportunities, from short strolls from your car to longer exploratory walks in quiet remote places.

Initially founded for public recreation in 1959, this area was further protected as a national park in 1967. Since then the park has grown to over 11,000 hectares. Much of the park's personality is derived from the Hawkesbury Sandstone that defines much of the landscape, but the park also still hosts the rich history of the traditional owners, with many engravings, paintings and other significant sites within the park boundaries. The walks in this chapter have been chosen to showcase the diverse scenery of the park – they even include the Mt Ettalong walk, just outside the park boundary, but providing sweeping vistas over the park and surrounding areas.

# 17 Mt Ettalong Lookout

This lovely short walk, actually just outside Brisbane Water National Park, leads you along an old trail to two fenced lookouts with wide sweeping views. A picnic table among the Sydney Red Gums, just before the two main lookouts, makes a good spot for a snack. The lookouts provide views over Umina Beach, Brisbane Water, Bouddi National Park, Pearl Beach and out to the Pacific Ocean.

### At a glance

**Grade:** Easy

**Time:** 30 mins

**Distance:** 1.4 km return

**Ascent/descent:** 30 metres ascent/descent

**Conditions:** Best views on sunny days or just before sunset

**Getting there:**

**Car:** Drive along Patonga Dr to the car park next to the large water tank, about 200 metres before Pearl Beach Dr – the driveway is marked with a small Mt Ettalong Lookout sign

**GPS of start/end:** -33.5363, 151.3061

## Walk directions

1 From the car park, follow the management trail around the water tank and then around the locked gate. The trail leads you through the bush, passing a few painted *Lookout* signs and past some Sydney Red Gums (ignoring the few side tracks leading to informal unfenced views). Continue to walk along the top of the ridge until you come to

a turning circle and the end of the management trail, where you will find a picnic table.

2 The walk continues uphill along a narrower track and over the rocky platform. Continue walking along the top of the ridge until you come to the *Lookouts* sign with two arrows.

3 From the intersection turn right to check out Pearl Beach Lookout, then head back to the main path and continue along the ridge, following the left-hand arrow on the *Lookouts* sign, and ducking under the Red Gum branch. You will soon climb up a short ramp to the fenced Mt Ettalong Lookout, with its grand views. A metal compass plaque helps identify the major landmarks in the view.

4 Return the way you came.

Pearl Beach and Lion Island from Mt Ettalong

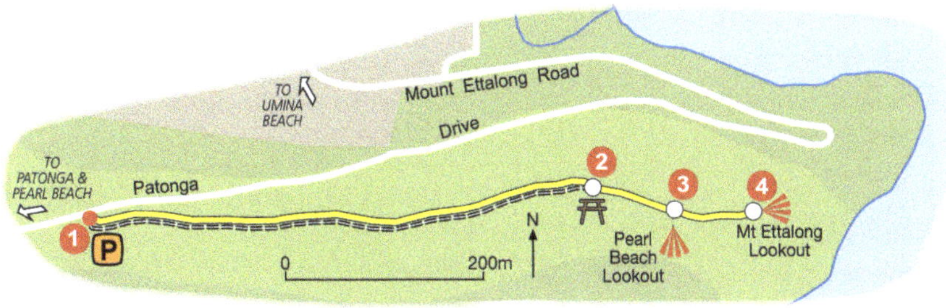


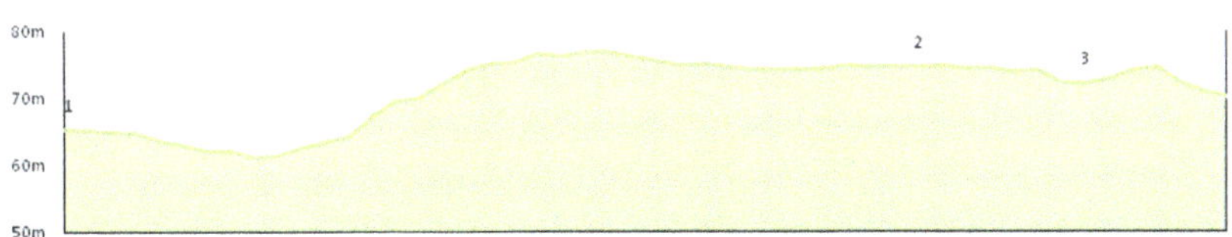

# 18 Patonga to Pearl Beach

Patagona Village is a small township on the Hawkesbury River, and near the ferry wharf you will find the Eve Williams Memorial Oval, which houses a large pavilion, drinking water and public toilets. Here you can also find fish and chips and basic supplies, or duck into Patonga Beach Hotel for a cold drink at the bar or meal on the deck. From Patonga, this walk takes you up a track, following the Great North Walk through part of Brisbane Water National Park, and via Warrah Lookout along the wide trail down to Pearl Beach for lunch at the café or a dip at the beach. Enjoy the wildflowers in spring and also the water views on sunny days. Pearl Beach itself is long and crescent-shaped, with rocky points at either end. At the southern end you can find an ocean pool while the northern end has the old Pearl Beach Road carved through the rock. The beach is popular with swimmers but you should note that there are no surf life savers.

## At a glance

**Grade:** Medium

**Time:** 1 hr 30 mins

**Distance:** 4.2 km one way

**Ascent/descent:** 180 metres ascent/descent

**Conditions:** Anytime - best views on sunny days

**Getting there:**

**Ferry:** River postman from Brooklyn - 1330 Mon to Thu, 1100 and 1330 weekends (times may change, confirm on T 9985 7566)

**Bus:** Take the Busways no. 52\0 from Woy Woy station - 0806, 1112 and 1508 weekdays, 0935 and 1305 Sat, 1535 Sun

**Car:** Drive into Patonga along Patonga Dr - parking near the wharf and in nearby streets

**Return:** Retrace your steps back to the start or take the Busways no. 52\0 bus to Woy Woy station (0715, 0742, 0843, 1145, 1545 and 1639 Mon-Fri; 0724 1027, 1345, Sat; 1136 and 1636 Sun)

**GPS of start:** -33.5504, 151.2746

**GPS of end:** -33.5444, 151.3071

## Walk directions

**1** From the Patonga wharf car park, head along the foreshore, keeping the water on the right. Soon you'll come to the Warrah Reserve boat ramp, which provides a large car park and access to both the ramp and Patonga Beach, as well as garbage bins, picnic table and information board.

**2** Continue along the beach until, just before the very end, you'll see the *Brisbane Water National Park* sign. This area of the beach is also known as 'Dark Corner'.

**3** Follow the *Warrah Trig 1.7km* sign up the steps. The track winds up the side of the hill, soon turning left and following the ridge line uphill. After heading up some stairs alongside a large rock, you will come to a lovely view across the water. Here, the track veers left and climbs up more steps before flattening out. Just after passing two GNW arrows next to each other (at the end of a large crack in the rock), the track passes some large Sydney Red Gums and comes to an unfenced rock platform on the right with a sweeping Broken Bay view, an informal and unfenced vantage point at the top of the cliffs.

**4** Continue to follow the Great North Walk arrows gently uphill along the track, which winds gently through the bush, passing the occasional glimpse of water to the right. After a short time, the track comes to a clear intersection with the Pearl Beach/Patonga fire trail, with a sign pointing back to *Patonga* (make a mental note of this spot if retracing your steps later).

**5** At the intersection, turn right and follow the Great North Walk arrow downhill along the wide management trail. The trail passes a track on the right to an unfenced view (marked with 5 large boulders) before coming to an intersection near the Warrah Lookout, and a sign pointing back to *Patonga*. Turn right and head between the timber posts, following the path for about 70 metres before coming to the fenced Warrah Lookout. Views here look out over the Hawkesbury River, and from left to right you can see the escarpment forming

# 18 Patonga to Pearl Beach

the southern boundary of Brisbane Water National Park, out to the ocean, Barrenjoey Head, West Head, along Cowan Creek, Juno Point and towards Patonga. Retrace your steps to the managemant trail.

**6** Follow the *Pearl Beach* sign downhill along the management trail. The trail leads down the hill and bends right soon after passing some filtered water views over Pearl Beach. You will then gently wind down around the side of a steep gully and, shortly after passing between two large rocks, the trail rounds a left-hand bend, just below a long cliff face with several sandstone caves. These make up Pearl Caves, one of which houses a few small columns, stalagmites and stalactites growing at the back. For your own safety and that of the caves, these are best viewed at a distance.

**7** Continue downhill along the management trail. There is a distinct change in vegetation as the trail winds down the hill and about 100 metres after seeing the first house, you will head around a locked gate and a *Pearl Beach/ Patonga* fire trail sign to find Crystal Street (again make a mental note of this spot if retracing your steps later).

**8** Turn right and walk along the dirt road. After it becomes sealed take the first left into Diamond Road. This heads over Green Point Creek (with a detailed risk warning sign). Turn right into Tourmaline Avenue and you will soon come to some shops and a left turn into Pearl Parade, at the front of a café (open 7 days for breakfast, lunch and dinners) and general store. Across the road is Pearl Beach and a children's playground. Those in search of a more refined dining experience should try *Pearls on the Beach*, on the other side of the road (Thursday to Sunday for lunch and dinner, T 4342 4400).

Warrah Lookout

9 Follow Pearl Parade, keeping the beach to the right, and you'll soon come to the bus stop, then a toilet block and a wide entrance to Pearl Beach (almost opposite Amethyst Ave).

# 19 Little Wobby to Woy Woy

Crossing the middle of Brisbane Water National Park, this walk has several highlights including Rocky Ponds. Starting with a ferry trip from Brooklyn, the walk follows a series of faint tracks, clear tracks and management trails. You will enjoy a range of panoramic views from Tumblecow II ridge, Rocky Ponds (Tank Creek) and an optional side trip to enjoy the view from Mount Wondabyne. The ponds are a series of cascades, waterholes and falls at the lower end of the creek, flowing over a wide, solid rock bed of a reddish colour. There are several small overhangs and ponds carved into the rock, and this spot provides a good place to cool down on a hot day. The walk finishes with some contrast beside the Woy Woy landfill and a road walk to Woy Woy Station. Make sure you leave enough time to get to the landfill gate before it is locked, or consider camping overnight at Tank Creek or Mt Wondabyne.

It is important to note that you need a permit to walk on the land housing the Broken Bay Sport and Recreation Centre, which belongs to the Department of Sport and Recreation. They are welcoming of bushwalkers and have an easy permission system in place. Permission can be obtained by calling (02) 4349 0600, after which they will email you a permit. Also note that you need to reach waypoint 11 by 4 pm (5 pm weekdays).

## At a glance

**Grade:** Hard

**Time:** 6 hrs 30 mins

**Distance:** 16.1 km one way

**Ascent/descent:** 590 metres ascent/600 metres descent

**Conditions:** The views are most spectacular on sunny days

**Getting there:**

**Train:** Hawkesbury River (Brooklyn) Station, return via train from Woy Woy

**Car:** Drive to the end of Brooklyn Rd (Brooklyn), turn left down Dangar Rd to Hawkesbury River Station – large parking area and more along Dangar Rd (note, some spots have time restrictions)

**Ferry:** The ferry wharf is right by the station; ferries leave every hour or two – check current times at www.hawkesburyriverferries.com.au (search Dangar Island), T 9985 7566; $6 one-way; running times can be weather-affected

**Water taxis:** Around $100 per group of 4; bookings usually required; Hawkesbury River Water Taxi, T0400 600 111 or Rick, T 0448 101 010

**GPS of start:** -33.5465, 151.2272

**GPS of end:** -33.4858, 151.3236

## Walk directions

1 From the Brooklyn ferry wharf, start the walk by catching the ferry or a water taxi to Little Wobby.

2 The town of Little Wobby, established during World War II to support artillery batteries and to prevent the Japanese from entering Broken Bay, is a boat-access only township on the eastern bank of the Hawkesbury River. The houses stretch along the river and are backed by the cliff line known as Tumblecow II. From the public wharf and phone box at Little Wobby beach, turn and head along the grassy edge in front of the houses. Follow the path as it heads up some stairs and under some houses before making its way around, generally following the shoreline. Soon after the large clearing, you will come to the Little Wobby Sport and Recreation Centre wharf.

3 Continue up the hill along the management trail, passing the boat ramp and keeping the water on the right. After a while the trail flattens out and passes a large concrete water tank on Croppy Point. Continue along the trail, heading more gently uphill and passing many water views. Eventually the trail bends left, passing an access track to Spring Beach on the right. This southwest facing yellow sand beach can be a good spot to stop and rest. Back on the trail you will come to an intersection with a track on the left moments later.

view from Tumblecow II

Top of the last fall on Tanks Creek

4 Take this left turn and head steeply up the faint *Defile Track,* past two sandstone caves. Once on the other side of the caves, follow the still faint track up the side of a gully which

soon passes around the roots of a large fallen tree. About 80 metres past the tree, tend left up through the rocky gully, keeping the rock wall and overhang on the right. Then follow the faint track as it winds up the ridge, veering right onto the main ridge. Near the top, you will pass some faint false tracks on the left before coming to a clear three-way intersection with the Midway Trail.

**5** Turn left and follow the main track north along the ridge. The track soon comes to another, more obvious three-way intersection where you veer right and then pass under some power lines. Follow the clear track through the scrub for a while, passing

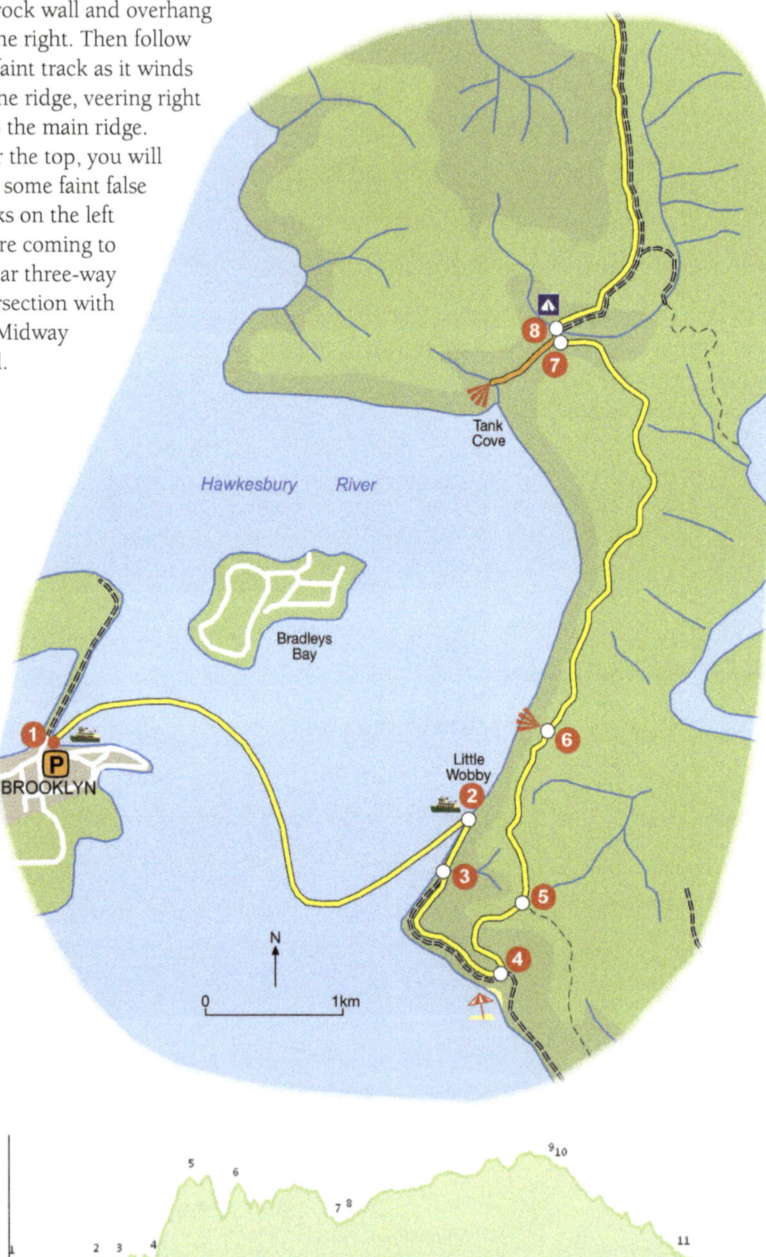

a few vantage points with extensive views over Brooklyn, before coming to another view by two TV antennas mounted on small masts. From here, continue along the track for another 350 metres, passing some more views and coming to two more TV antennas on another rocky outcrop. About 70 metres past these antennas, you will come to a large flat rock platform with yet another two antennas and wide views over Brooklyn and the Hawkesbury River. This is the Tumblecow II flat rock viewpoint.

6 Continue north, back into the bush. At length the track veers right, leaving the cliff top to round the hill known as Big Ben. Continue on, winding through the bush for some time, and passing a view to Patonga Creek on the right. After climbing down some rocks and through the thick heath, the track opens up onto a large rock platform and crosses the first creek (Tank Creek) before coming to an intersection with a track on the right, leading to Woy Woy.

7 Follow this track as it heads up the main creek (Tank Creek) for a few metres where you'll soon find a clear track through the heath, heading north. The track leads you into a small gully, on the other side of which you will come to a tree with exposed roots. Turn right and head upstream through the gully. After a few metres, turn left to follow an eroded track until

## Walk variation - Tank Creek last fall

From waypoint 7 (the rock platform on Tank Creek), head across the rest of the rock platform and follow the track downstream through the bush, keeping the main creek to the left. After about 100 metres you will find a short track on the left, leading to a view of Jeanie's Pool. Continue along the main track, past a sandstone boulder (ignoring a track on the left) then down the rock to come to an intersection. The short track on the left leads to Jeannie's Pool - well worth the visit. The northern side of the pool has an overhang nurturing a mossy environment and the pool is half-surrounded by cliffs, creating a fall to the pool below. Returning to the main track, continue away from the main rock wall and through the grass trees. You will soon pass another short track (on the left, leading to a rock pool) and soon come to the creek edge and a large sandstone platform. This is the top of the last waterfall on Tank Creek before the water flows into Tank Cove on the main river. From here you can see up the Hawkesbury past Dangar Island into Porto Bay. Just upstream is a series of cascades known as Allison's cascade. Retrace your steps back to waypoint 7.

you find a small clearing and a wider sandy trail. Follow this trail for about 50 metres to a three-way intersection. (The track on the left leads to the Tank Creek Campsite.)

Campsite

**8** From the intersection, continue along the main sandy track, gently uphill through the heath. After about 250 metres, the track widens into an old management trail and crosses a small creek. The trail continues to wind up the hill and is quite eroded in places. At the top of the rise, the old trail heads down through a gully and joins with a much wider management trail. Continue along this wider trail, ignoring the one on the right. After about 750 metres, you will climb a short but steep hill. At the top, follow the trail as it winds more gently uphill and crosses a long sandstone platform. After about 1.3 kilometres you'll come to a 'T' intersection and a sign pointing back to *Rocky Ponds Trail*.

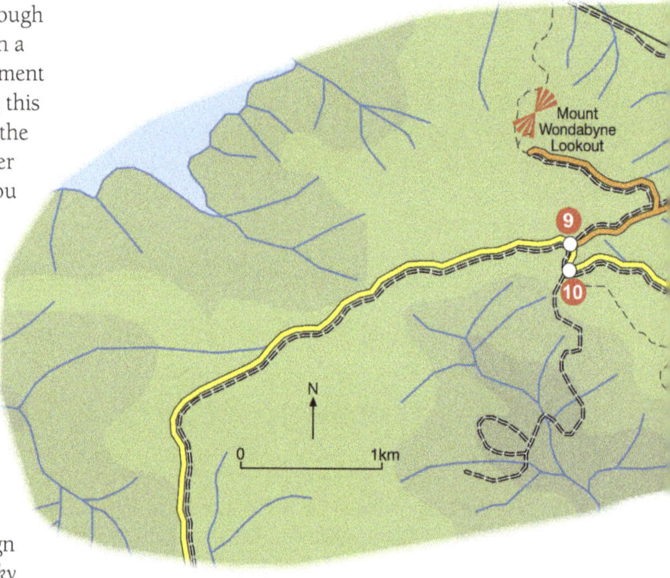


**9** Turn right, following the *Patonga* sign around the gate and down the gentle hill, coming to a 'T' intersection with another management trail 200 metres later.

**10** Turn left, following the management trail to another intersection, with a *Patonga* sign pointing to the right along the Great North Walk track. From here, continue straight, following the management trail east, down the long, gentle hill as it gradually steepens to wind down alongside the Woy Woy Landfill site. Near the front of the landfill, head through the gap in the fence and turn left onto the

## Walk variation - Mount Wondabyne Peak

From waypoint 9, turn left and follow the Girrakool sign along the management trail. After about 500 metres turn left and follow the Mt Wondabyne sign uphill along the trail. You will eventually come to a large clearing (turning circle) at the base of the rock wall - this is the Mount Wondabyne Campsite. Turn right, following the Mooney Mooney rest area sign along the track for about 90 metres before turning right again onto the unsignposted Mount Wondabyne peak track. This is flat at first, but starts to climb up a series of rock ledges. Soon you will pass a small cave, continuing up through a grove of small trees to come to the first peak. Continue along the ridge to the main peak and trig station. After enjoying the panoramic views, retrace your steps back to waypoint 9.

landfill driveway. Follow the driveway downhill for about 1 kilometre to the front gates on Nagari Road (these gates are locked after 1700 - 1600 on weekends - so make sure you allow plenty of time).

**11** From the landfill gates, turn right and follow Nagari Road, keeping the train tracks to your left. After nearly 3 kilometres you will pass a shopping centre and finally come to Woy Woy train station.

# 20 Staples Lookout to Mt Wondabyne Loop

Starting and finishing at Staples Lookout on Woy Woy Road, this walk follows sections of the Great North Walk around Mount Wondabyne and the old Bulls Hill Quarry. There are a few options for short side trips, one leading to the tranquil Kariong Brook falls and the other to the peak of Mount Wondabyne, which provides great views over the National Park to Woy Woy.

## At a glance

**Grade:** Medium

**Time:** 4 hrs 30 mins

**Distance:** 10.8 km circuit

**Ascent/descent:** 340 metres ascent/descent

**Conditions:** All seasons.

**Getting there:**

**Car:** Drive to Staples Lookout on Woy Woy Rd about 4.5 km south of Kariong

**GPS of start/end:** -33.4717, 151.2883

## Walk directions

**1** From Staples Lookout, walk downhill alongside Woy Woy Road (keeping the views to your left), crossing the road at some point where safe. Just after passing a large brown *Scenic Lookout 300m* sign, you come to the signposted start of *Thommo's Loop Fire Trail* and a locked gate.

**2** Turn right and head down the management trail. After a short while, you will come to an intersection with the power line service trail. Go straight ahead, following the *Thommo's Loop* sign. Follow this management trail as it winds down the hill and crosses a rock platform with good views. Continue along the management trail down the hill to a signposted three-way intersection with a *Staples Lookout* sign pointing back up the hill.

**3** Veer left and follow the *Patonga* sign. After winding down the hill for some time, you will come to a long rock platform, offering great views of Mt Wondabyne to your right. Continue to the far end of this platform, where you will find a signposted 'Y' intersection with a sign pointing back to *Girrakool*.

**4** Follow the *Patonga* sign, taking the narrower right-hand track. At the bottom of the hill, cross some boardwalks and continue up the other side, passing under the power lines.

**5** At a 'T' intersection, with a a sign pointing back to *Girrakool*, turn right, following the *Mt Wondabyne* sign along the management trail. Walk up a gentle slope to another signposted intersection and turn left, following the *Mt Wondabyne* sign up the rocky track. You will pass a Great North Walk walkers' register and then, after passing Mount Wondabyne on the left, you will come to an intersection with the Mt Wondabyne peak track (also on the left).

**6** Veer right and walk south, following the track up a small rise. After a short distance, you will come to a clearing at the end of a management trail, with a sign pointing back to *Mooney Mooney* rest area. This is the Mount Wondabyne campsite, which has an established fire circle but no water or other facilities.

# 20 Staples Lookout to Mt Wondabyne Loop

**7** Veer left here and follow the management trail down the hill, taking in some good views of Mount Wondabyne, Woy Woy and to Brisbane Water.

**8** Turn left at the intersection (with the Tunnel Track) and follow the management trail down the hill, passing a filtered view of the Woy Woy landfill site and some nice sandstone formations. Continue along the trail into a valley, crossing an often dry creek using a concrete ford. Soon after this, you come to a sign pointing back to *Tunnel Track* at a four-way intersection with some power lines.

**9** Continue straight and walk northeast along the management trail up the hill, away from the power lines (not following any of the signs). You will soon come to a three-way intersection, signposted *Thommo's Loop* to the left. Veer right, following the red-gravelly trail north as it winds gently downhill. Soon after passing an old rusty trailer on the left, you will pass a *Brisbane Water National Park* sign and go around a locked gate.

**10** Continue along the management trail. You will soon discover the old Bulls Hill Quarry which, in 2005, was worked upon by the then-Department of Land and Water Conservation to improve water flow quality from the sediment dams on the site. Continue around the edge, passing the pondage area (there are many tracks in the area – this walk follows the main Tunnel Track). Follow the trail as it bends left, rounding the quarry, crossing the

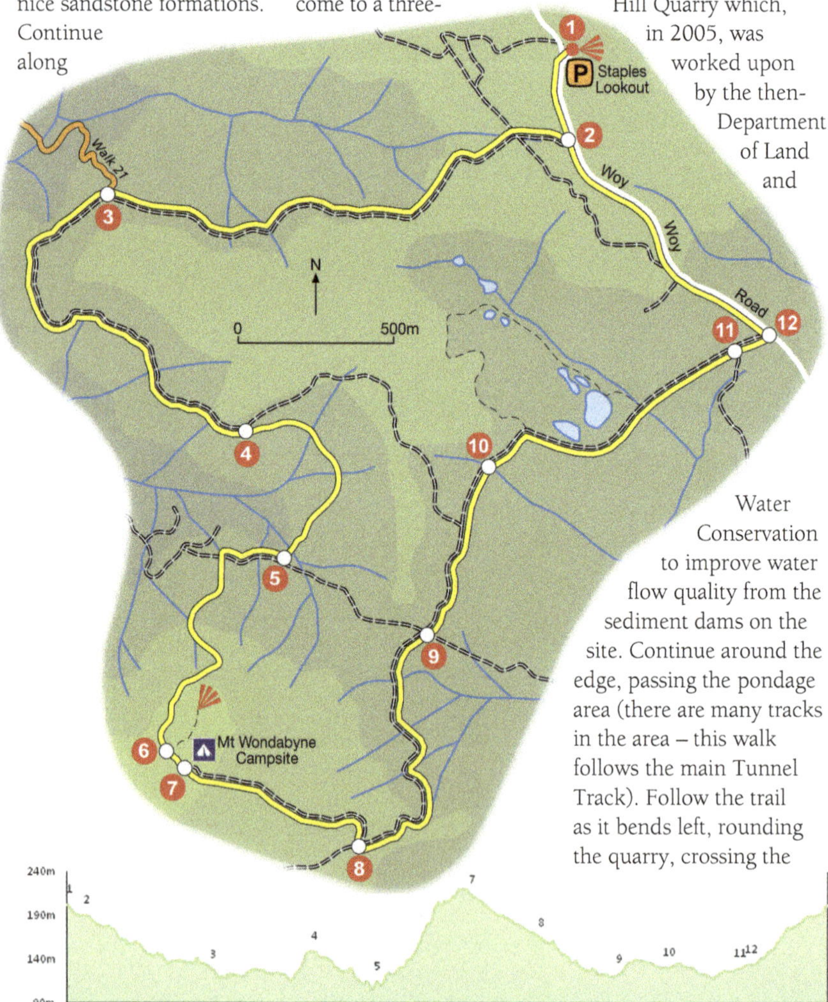

Trig on Mt Wondabyne

sandstone rock platform and climbing the trail. At length you will come to an intersection with a power line maintenance trail on the right, signposted 830.

**11** Go straight ahead towards the gate (and road) just visible up the gentle hill. On the other side of the gate, you will come to small clearing beside Woy Woy Road, a short distance uphill from the speed camera.

**12** Turn left and follow the road away from the speed camera. Soon after passing the large *Overtaking lane 400m Ahead* sign, you will come to a *Roy Lamb the Sand Man* sign. Continue up the hill for quite some distance until you come to an intersection signposted as the start of the *Thommo's Loop Fire Trail*, with a gate on the left (just before the brown Scenic Lookout sign). You are now back at waypoint 2. Retrace your steps back to Staples Lookout.

## Mount Wondabyne Peak

Mount Wondabyne is one of the most prominent peaks in Brisbane Water National Park. The long cone-shaped hill has a rocky top and is home to a trig station. To the east are good views over the Brisbane Water, Woy Woy and other central coast suburbs and to the west, down next to Mullet Creek, you can see some buildings near Wondabyne Station and the train line. Otherwise, most of the expansive views are over much of Brisbane Water National Park. There are some small trees providing limited shade, making this a great place to soak up the views.

To get to the peak itself, turn left from waypoint 6 and follow the track northeast as it heads towards the hill. Follow the track as it climbs up a series of rock ledges, then passes a small cave (suitable for 2 or 3 campers). After arriving at the first peak, continue along the ridge to the next peak, where you will find the trig point and its 360-degree views.

# 21 Staples Lookout to Kariong Brook

This walk provides the shortest access to Kariong Brook waterfall, one of the most picturesque falls in the area. It begins at Staples Lookout on Woy Woy Road (built as a tribute to Charles J. Staples, a pioneer of the route that Woy Woy Road now follows), which provides good views east across the Central Coast, the Brisbane Water and out into the ocean. At the lookout is a large car park and picnic tables, with plenty of natural shade. An inscription at the lookout quotes Psalm 119:27: 'and I shall meditate on your wondrous works'. Most of the walking is along the Thommo's Loop management trail, except for the last descent into Kariong Brook. The waterfall is a cool place to stop for lunch on a warm day.

### At a glance

**Grade:** Medium

**Time:** 2 hrs 30 mins

**Distance:** 5.7 km return

**Ascent/descent**: 230 metres ascent/descent

**Conditions:** All seasons, waterfall is best after some rain

**Getting there:**

**Car:** Drive to Staples Lookout on Woy Woy Rd, about 4.5 km south of Kariong

**GPS of start/end:** -33.4717, 151.2883

# 21 Staples Lookout to Kariong Brook

## Walk directions

First, follow the notes for waypoints 1 and 2 of walk 20 (page 99).

**3** Turn right at the intersection, following the Girrakool sign along the narrower track. Walk down the hill, passing a rock outcrop on the left, until you come to a clearing that has been used as a campsite. From the clearing, continue down the hill, stepping down the rocks. Turn right at a handrail and walk down the rocky track, along some rock walls. Near the bottom of the valley, you will pass under a sandstone overhang and get a glimpse of Kariong Brook. Continue down and cross the creek in front of the pool and falls. After rain, these falls can become spectacular and at other times can offer a cool place to rest.

**4** Return the way you came.

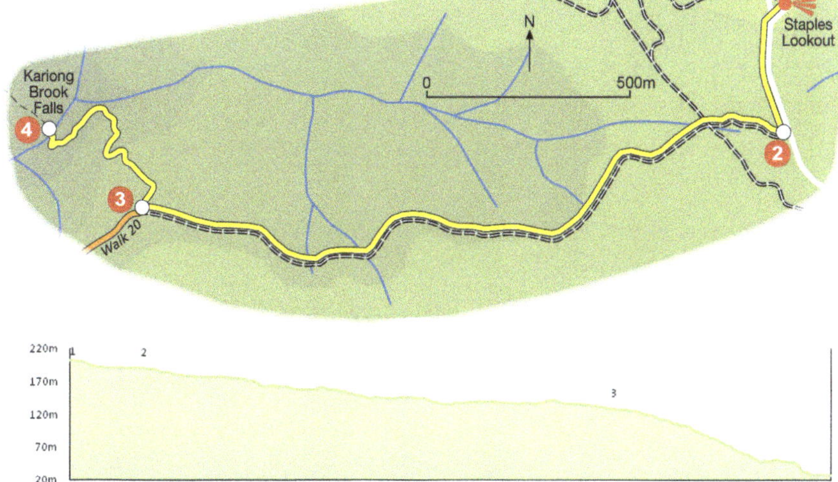

# 22 Pindar Cave

Pindar Lookout, Pool and Cave are the most impressive features of this remarkable walk, with each feature deserving of its own unique track. The walk takes off from the tiny Wondabyne Station (built in 1889 when it was known as Mullet Creek Station) before climbing onto the plateau and along the ridge line to Mt Pindar. The Wondabyne area is defined by the National Park's flora and fauna, the railway station and the quarry, which produced sandstone building materials used in the construction of Canberra's National War Memorial and was reopened in 2000 for the restoration of St Mary's Cathedral spire in Sydney. The walk passes over rocky terrain with many spider webs across the track. Unless you come by water, the only access is by train – there is no other vehicular access.

## At a glance

**Grade:** Hard

**Time:** 4 hrs 30 mins

**Distance:** 11.5 km return

**Ascent/descent:** 490 metres ascent/descent

**Conditions:** All seasons

**Getting there:**
**Train:** Catch the train to Wondabyne and let the guard know you want to get off at Wondabyne Station, otherwise the train will not stop. Travel in the last carriage as the platform is very short. To catch the train after the walk, wave to the driver from the platform.

**GPS of start/end:** -33.4921, 151.257

Pindar Cave

## Walk directions

1 From Wondabyne Station, follow the Great North Walk signs to the base of the large hill then climb up some rock steps, passing a large boulder on the left. Continue up the hill for a while before climbing some more steps that have been cut into a rock ledge.

2 Continue through a clearing with an old fire place, following the management trail up the hill and past the *Brisbane Water National Park* signpost. After a short distance, the trail bends to the right and continues up the long hill to the intersection with the Pindar Cave management trail, with a rocky clearing on the left.

3 Turn left and follow the management trail to the west, keeping the large rocky outcrop to the right. Follow the trail as it narrows into a track and undulates for some time through some rocky and dense scrub. Eventually you will swing around to the north and arrive at the Mt Pindar Lookout, indicated by arrows marked in the surface of the rock. There are views from here over the Mooney Mooney township and creek.

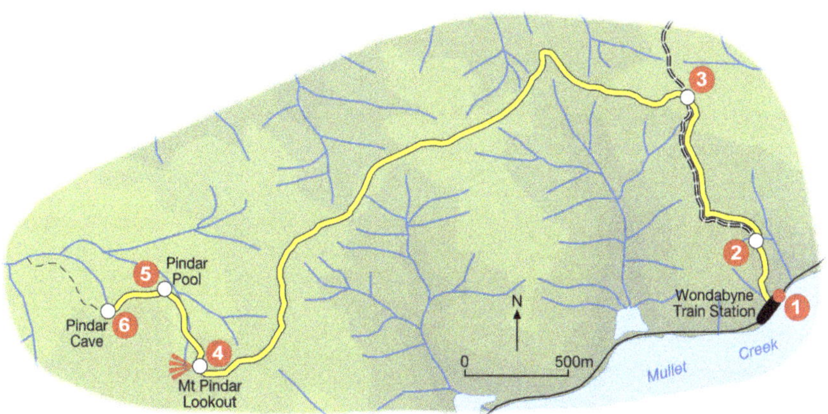


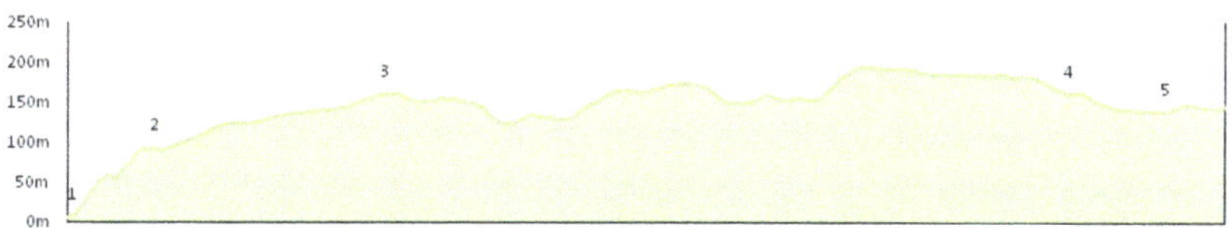

**4** Continue along the bush track, heading north, around the edge of the ridge. You will soon descend into the valley below, continuing through areas of thick vegetation, until you emerge into a clearing next to Pindar Pool, a 10 by 5 metre tub. When full it is surrounded by birdlife.

**5** Turn left at the pool and follow the track west into a small, sandy clearing. Continue along the track as it bends right, below a rocky outcrop on the left, and follows the rocky outcrop for approximately 100 metres to the large overhang of Pindar Cave. The floor of the cave can be used for a nap, the roof blackened from many campfires belonging to overnight guests.

**6** Return the way you came.

## Walk variation – Pindar Waterfall

If you fancy exploring a little more, continue straight ahead at Pindar Cave, parallel to the rocky outcrop. After following the cliff line for a little while, follow the bush track as it bends slightly to the right and heads northwest, crossing several rocky outcrops and going down towards the creek line. You will drop down past some rock shelves to the waterfall, formed by a vegetation-enclosed stream which runs over and through a rocky outcrop. Retrace your steps back to waypoint 6.

# 23 Bulgandry Engravings

Named after Bulgandry man, an ancestral hero and the subject of one of the more detailed engravings at the site, the Bulgandry Engravings is clearly a special place. The walk is accessible for people in wheelchairs but it is important to note the path has deteriorated in some places, making it a bit bouncy.

## At a glance

**Grade:** Easy – Wheelchair accessible (a bit rough in places)

**Time:** 20 mins

**Distance:** 800 metres return

**Ascent/descent:** 20 metres ascent/descent

**Conditions:** The engravings are clearest on sunny days when the sun is low in the sky and soon after rain.

**Getting there:**
**Car:** Drive along Woy Woy Rd for 2.8 km from Central Coast Hwy, and along the short dirt driveway signposted *Bulgandry*

**GPS of start/end:** -33.456, 151.2844

# 23 Bulgandry Engravings

## Walk directions

1 From the Bulgandry car park, follow the NPWS arrow through the timber chicane and along the footpath. The path winds gently through the bush with some distant valley views to the left and a spectacular wildflower display (in spring). You will pass three interesting information signs before coming to an intersection and *Care of the Site* sign just before the actual engraving site. The engravings have been here for centuries if not millennia, so please stay on the boardwalk to avoid accidental damage – simply

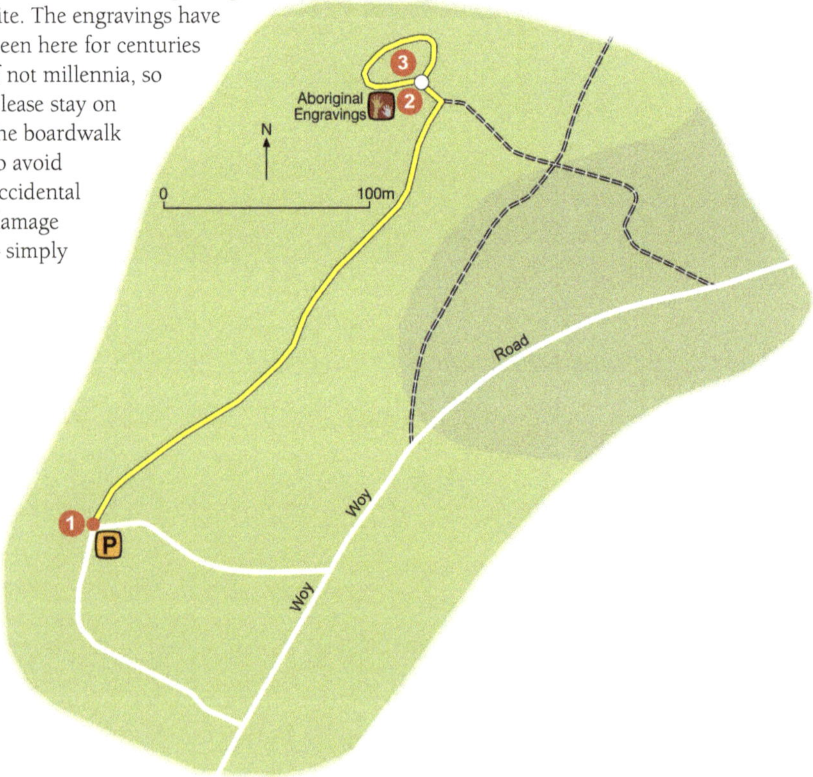

touching the engravings can exacerbate the weathering process.

**2** Walk down the hill to the timber platform and turn right to head anticlockwise around the rock platform. There are numbered signs (2-10) on the path that provide some details on the individual engravings. The last engraving (number 10) is that of a man, Bulgandry, an ancestral hero. The NPWS has marked the engravings as follows: 1: A fish (plaque now missing). 2: Another fish. 3: Eel. 4: Dolphin (or large fish). 5: Woman and kangaroo. 6: Speared fish. 7: Kangaroo and octopus (?). 8: Axe grinding grooves. 9: Canoe (?). 10: Bulgandry man.

**3** Return the way you came.

# 24 Girrakool Loop track

This loop walk begins at the well-established Girrakool picnic area, named after the Aboriginal word meaning 'place of still waters'. Only 5 minutes' drive from Kariong, the area is suitable for families: facilities at the site are ample, including barbecues, tables, shelters, water and toilets. Dedicated to John 'Jack' Higgs, the first superintendent of Brisbane Water National Park, and Mrs Vera Murdoch, who provided the funds for its establishment, this is National Park territory and so appropriate fees apply. There are four lookouts and an Aboriginal engravings site along the walk, plus it offers a couple of side trips, visiting some good spots on Piles Creek. The views from each of the lookouts are filtered through trees, but still worth the visit. The walk is especially nice in late winter and early spring, when the wildflowers are blooming.

## At a glance

**Grade:** Medium

**Time:** 45 mins

**Distance:** 1.4 km circuit

**Ascent/descent:** 60 metres ascent/descent

**Conditions:** All seasons.

Getting there:

**Car:** Turn off Pacific Hwy into Quarry Rd, Somersby and follow signs to Girrakool picnic area

**GPS of start/end:** -33.4317, 151.2766

## Walk directions

**1** From the Girrakool picnic area information sign, walk across the car park to the *Girrakool Loop 2km* signpost on the other side. Follow this into the bush, leaving the freeway noise behind. Cross a rock platform then go down a series of steps, coming to a large rock platform with a pine log and *Aboriginal Site* sign. The engravings on this rock have faded, but with a bit of effort you can make out a man and kangaroo (remember not to walk on the engravings as this will erode them further). The cliff edge around the rock is un-fenced.

**2** Walk down the stairs that lead through the crack at the lower end of the rock platform and wind through the bush for a little while. Soon after passing a glimpse of Piles Creek to the left, you'll come to a 'T' intersection, marked with a small arrow sign post pointing to the right.

**3** Turn right, following the arrow along the wide track (keeping the valley to the left) to *Broula Lookout*. The lookout is fenced and thicker with trees that it must once have been, when it offered a vantage point for the Piles Creek waterfall. 'Broula' is an Aboriginal word referring to a place of trickling water.

**4** Turn right here and follow the clearer track heading directly away from the cliff, to a 'T' intersection with the *Girrakool Loop* footpath. Turn left and follow the *Girrakool Loop* sign along the stone path and walk down the steps to *Illoura Lookout*. Here you will have a filtered view up and down the Leask and Piles Creek junction, with a glimpse of a waterfall at Piles Creek. 'Illoura' is an Aboriginal word referring to a pleasant or peaceful place

**5** Turn right at the lookout, following the *Girrakool Loop* sign and keeping the green fence to the left. Walk up the steps and go straight ahead at the intersection, following the *Girrakool Loop* sign up the rocky track. Pass the old *lookout* sign, then after crossing a small timber footbridge, continue along the track as it winds through the bush for a little while

before crossing another footbridge with a handrail. A short distance later, you will cross a longer timber bridge, then walk up the hill to an intersection, with Andamira Lookout (an un-signposted side trip) a short distance to the left.

**6** Turn sharp right at the intersection and walk up the timber steps.

At the top of the steps is *Boondi Lookout*. The view here is mostly of the trees in the valley, with some glimpses of Leask Creek to the right. 'Boondi' is a word used by the Darkinjung people meaning 'club-headed weapon'.

**7** From the lookout, walk up the stairs, following the main track as it flattens and gently winds through the bush, across a rock platform and across a small wooden bridge. Soon after leaving the power lines, you will come to a fence and the top of Girrakool Picnic area. Walk through the picnic area, tending left to the car park.

Piles Creek Cascades

## Walk side trips – Piles Creek Cascades and Waterfall

**Piles Creek cascades:** from waypoint 3, turn left and follow the track in the opposite direction to the arrow, down the hill. Head over the rocks, through a small crack and around the red gum tree, to the rocky creek bed of Piles Creek. Here the creek flows across a rock platform, creating sink holes, small water holes and cascades. Care is needed as the rocks are slippery, and the area may not be passable after rain.

**Piles Creek Waterfall:** from waypoint 5, turn left, following the left-hand Piles Creek and GNW arrow down the wooden steps (keeping the valley to the right). You will soon pass a *Caution Low Water Level Crossing Only* sign and cross Piles Creek using concrete stepping stones (the creek may be impassable after rain). Follow the track until it opens up on an unfenced rock platform, at the top of the waterfall. Note the cliff edge is unfenced and dangerous to approach too close for the view. The Bundilla Lookout on the other side of the valley provides the only direct view onto the falls.

# 25 Piles Creek Loop

Starting from the Girrakool picnic area, this walk takes you on a round trip through a very beautiful part of the Brisbane Water National Park. The walk explores both sides of Piles Creek, rewarding you with its waterfalls and lookouts. Girrakool picnic area has BBQs and toilets.

### At a glance

**Grade:** Medium

**Time:** 2 hrs

**Distance:** 4.1 km circuit

**Ascent/descent:** 300 metres ascent/descent

**Conditions:** All seasons

**Getting there:**
**Car:** Turn off Pacific Hwy into Quarry Rd, Somersby, and follow signs to Girrakool picnic area

**GPS of start/end:** -33.4317, 151.2766

## Walk directions

1 From the lower side of the car park, follow the *To The Great North Walk* sign down the path to the lower picnic area. Walk past the toilet block (on your left). Continue through another picnic area and turn right, following the *Piles Creek Loop Track* sign down the steps. At an intersection with the Broula Lookout track on the left you can take a side trip to Broula Lookout, or carry on.

Phil Houghton Bridge over Piles Creek

**2** Follow the *Girrakool Loop* sign down along the stone path then down some steps to the fenced and signposted *Illoura Lookout*. This provides a view up and down the Leask and Piles Creek junction, with a glimpse of a waterfall at Piles Creek.

**3** Turn right at the lookout and follow the *Girrakool Loop* sign, keeping the green fence to your left. Head up some steps to a 'Y' intersection with a sign pointing back to *Girrakool Car Park*. Follow the *Piles Creek Loop* sign down the rocky steps (keeping the valley to the right) and you will soon cross Leask Creek on a narrow concrete foot bridge. Continue along the track as it winds gently through the bush and to an intersection with a track heading down to Bundilla Lookout on the left (another brief side trip).

**4** Follow the main track down the hill, keeping the valley (and lookout) to the left, then down some rocky steps and past a large rock wall on the right. Further downhill, you come close to a waterhole on Piles Creek. From here, head up the hill, passing more stone boulders, and then go down some steps next to another rock wall. You will pass a couple of metal arrow markers soon before coming to a large rock overhang at the top of a set of stairs. Here the Western Piles Creek Caves provide a sheltered spot for walkers to rest.

**5** From the cave, walk down the stairs, keeping the cave wall to the right. Follow the track

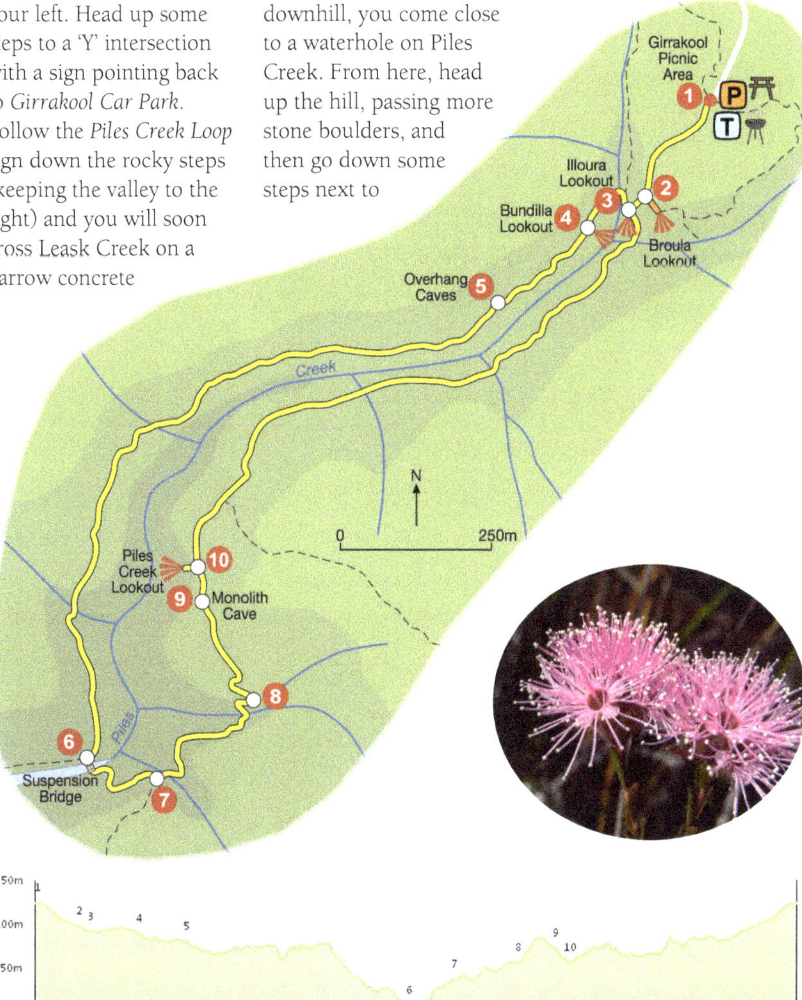

through the bush for a while, passing another rock wall and crossing over three small foot bridges. Pass a couple more caves and a rock wall and then some distant views, to the left. After passing another cave, cross the creek using the handrail and continue along a section of track with a steep drop to the left. Head down a long set of steps with an old handrail, and continue down the hill to a large clearing and the Phil Houghton suspension Bridge, which crosses Piles Creek and is part of the Great North Walk (it replaced an older bridge, part of which is still visible upstream). The bridge is quite stable and holds up to 8 people, offering views upstream and down.

**6** After crossing the bridge, turn left past the old bridge, then head right, up the hill. After a short way, where the track flattens out, you come to an intersection next to a small creek, with a *Great North Walk* sign pointing back to *Piles* Creek.

**7** Turn left and cross the small creek, then follow the *Girrakool* sign along the bush track as it winds up the side of the hill then heads back downhill into Rat Gully. Cross a boulder field and creek, with steps cut in the rock to help the crossing, and you will then pass the old bridge and head into the bush again. Follow the track when it does a right-hand switchback (at the *Girrakool* sign) and climb the small hill to an un-signposted lookout.

**8** Continue up the hill, initially keeping the large gully to the right. Veer left and head to the top of the hill, passing a large monolithic rock. After about 60 metres there's a similar rock with a large sandstone overhanging cave, just to the left of the track, known as Monolith Cave. Take great care when exploring the rock formations here.

**9** Go straight ahead at the cave, through the cleft in the rock, then follow the clear track past another rock wall and you will come to an intersection at the base of a timber staircase.

**10** After a brief trip to Piles Creek Lookout, walk up the wooden staircase, then along the track for a little while, until you come to a three-way intersection and a *Girrakool* sign. Veer left, following the *Girrakool* sign along the track. After a short time, you will pass under four sandstone overhangs and then cross a few small tributaries. The caves provide good shelter and a great spot to rest. Continue through thick scrub, until it opens up onto an unfenced rock platform at the top of Piles Creek Waterfall. Cross the creek using the concrete stepping stones (the creek may be impassable after rain), head up the wooden steps and you soon come to Illoura Lookout. You are now back at waypoint 3. Turn right at the Illoura Lookout, following the *Girrakool Loop* sign up the stone steps, and retrace your earlier steps back to the car park.

# Central West

The walks described in this chapter help you explore three very different reserves, a State Forest and two National Parks, each protecting a unique combination of flora, fauna, geology and waterways.

Strickland State Forest has been harvested in the past and is now a re-growth forest, but set aside for environmental protection, education and recreation. You get a real sense here of how fragile environments can be, but also how, with good care, they can recover well. You could spend the better part of a day here, enjoying the walks, the Bell birds, the diverse forests and picnic areas.

The Somersby Falls walk follows Floods Creek through a section of Brisbane Water National Park. Since this walk is different both in style and location from those in chapter 4 we thought it best fit here. Although a short walk, you can spend many hours enjoying both the beauty and with the great picnic facilities provided.

Popran National Park, like others in the area, is to a great extent defined by the sandstone. The park has five main pockets of land and protects some significant catchments of the Hawkesbury River. Here you will discover many tangled angophoras, ironbarks, turpentines, grey gums, Sydney peppermints and Sydney blue gums. In spring this park is alive with wildflowers, and this is an especially good time to visit.

# 26 Bellbird Trail

Plenty of the Strickland rainforest can be seen on this walk, as well as the tall trees of the arboretum found inside the forest. You are likely to have the sound of Bellbirds adding to the atmosphere along parts of this walk. There are a number of creek crossings along the way, one with a small suspension bridge. The Banksia picnic area is only a very short deviation off the road, if you want to make use of the facilities.

## At a glance

**Grade:** Medium

**Time:** 1 hr 15 mins

**Distance:** 3.3 km circuit

**Ascent/descent:** 90 metres ascent/descent

**Conditions:** All seasons; plenty of shade

**Getting there:**

**Car:** From Mangrove Rd, about 100 m south of the F3, turn into Strickland Rd at the signposted entrance to Strickland State Forest, then drive for about 2.6 km, following the signs, to the Lower Car Park

**GPS of start/end:** -33.3799, 151.3251

## Walk directions

**1** From the lower car park, follow the *Walking Trails* arrow along the management trail. The walk passes an information board with a map of the walking trails, and continues a short distance to an intersection just before the creek crossing.

**2** Cross the creek and follow the *Arboretum Loop Trail* arrow along the old management trail. You will meander through shaded forest, filled with cabbage palms, for 450 metres before reaching a signposted intersection.

**3** Veer left, following the *Arboretum Trail* down the timber steps and along the overgrown management trail. After a short distance, you will cross a suspension bridge over Narara Creek, then turn to the left and almost immediately reach an unmarked intersection with a narrow bush track on the right.

4 Ignore this and continue along the old management trail, away from the suspension bridge, until you come to an intersection.

5 Veer left, following the *Arboretum Loop* Trail arrow along the track, which will take you through a moist forest, filled with cabbage palms, with the creek visible to the left. You will cross over a number of fallen tree trunks with steps cut into them. At one point, you will pass a track marker arrow, where a large fallen tree trunk spans the creek, to the left. Soon after this, you will pass a *Forest Arboretum* information board. Continue along the track, following several track arrows until you reach an intersection with a management trail (with a gate visible to the left). There is a grove of tall Bunya Pine trees here.

6 Turn right, following the old management trail away from the nearby gate. After 220 metres you will come to a left-hand track, signposted *Bellbird Trail*.

7 Follow the *Bellbird Trail*, keeping an eye and ear out for the Bellbirds that live here – they are olive-green with a short yellow bill, a red-orange bare eye patch and orange-yellow feet and legs. Their call is described as a 'sweet, musical, bell-like "tink"'. There are some track markers on short brown posts in this area, although they are often obscured in the undergrowth. Follow the narrow, and sometimes faint, bush track as it goes through vine filled forest for a short distance before coming to a 'T' intersection, marked with a number of arrows. Turn left and follow the narrow bush track for some time through the ferns and vines. Narara Creek may often be visible just to the right. After a while, you will arrive at some concreted steps just before crossing Narara Creek. You might want to take a break here for lunch.

8 Cross Narara Creek and follow the bush track, which immediately bends to the right. You will meander through the forest for some time before reaching an intersection signposted *Return To Carpark*. You are now back at waypoint 3. Turn left, following the *Return To Carpark* arrow and retrace your steps to waypoint 2, then veer right, re-cross the creek and walk a short distance back to the car

## Central Coast environment – Strickland Forest

The Strickland State Forest has a wide range of vegetation, including patches of rainforest along the sheltered creeks. The walking tracks take in some beautiful scenery, including a mixture of native forest and the remnants of an old arboretum. This arboretum is one of the oldest in Australia, with plantings dating from 1887-1924. Numerous signs have been placed along the walking tracks to identify some of the species of trees, examples of Hoop Pine, Bunya Pine, Tallow Wood and Red Cedar.

# 27 Strickland Falls & Cabbage Tree Loop

### At a glance

**Grade:** Medium

**Time:** 1 hr 30 mins

**Distance:** 3 km circuit

**Ascent/descent:** 220 metres ascent/ descent

**Conditions:** suitable all year-round

**Getting there:**
**Car:** From Mangrove Rd, about 100m south of the F3, turn into Strickland Rd at the signposted entrance to Strickland State Forest, then drive for about 1.4 km, following the signs, to the Banksia Picnic Area

**GPS of start/end:** -33.3733, 151.3225

This loop walk combines the Strickland Falls and Cabbage Tree loop walks. It begins in the dry eucalypt forest around the Banksia Picnic Area and soon descends into rainforest remnants, filled with ferns and cabbage tree palms. The forest is no longer harvested but managed instead for education and recreation purposes, and the Friends of Strickland are responsible for projects such as the construction of walking tracks. Walkers should note that Strickland is open during the day only, between 7am and 5pm from April to October, and until 7pm from November to March. The walk includes some great scenery along the base of the cliff line and around the falls, although the falls themselves are often just a trickle, depending on recent rainfall. You could do a short return walk to Strickland Falls by retracing your steps from waypoint 3.

## Walk directions

**1** From the car park, follow the road away from the picnic area where you will soon reach an intersection with a bush track, signposted with *Strickland Falls* and *40 Minute Easy Walk*.

**2** Follow the bush track away from the road, passing the *Strickland Falls* signpost on your left. The track initially passes through quite dry forest. After a while, you will pass some rock overhangs and continue along the track as it descends through increasingly moist forest and boulders, to reach the signposted *Strickland Falls*, 740 metres from waypoint 2. These will be most impressive after good rain.

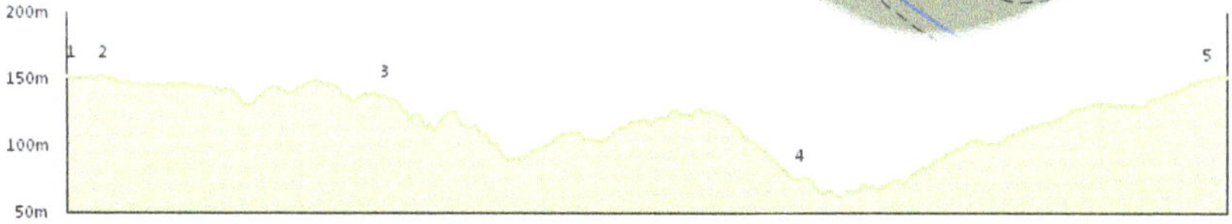

Strickland Falls
3
0
250m
N
TO MANGROVE RD & PACIFIC HWY
2
1
P
Strickland
STRICKLAND STATE FOREST
5
T
4
Road

200m
150m
100m
50m
1 2
3
4
5

## 27 Strickland Falls & Cabbage Tree Loop

**3** Turn left at the waterfall intersection, going down the gentle hill. The track meanders through some beautiful scenery with ferns, cabbage palms and boulders. After a while, you will cross a gully below some imposing cliffs. Continue on to an intersection signposted *Cabbage Tree Trail*. Veer right, following the *Cabbage Tree Trail* arrow. This section of the walk passes some boulders and continues through forest filled with cabbage palms and ferns. Follow the track until you reach an intersection, signposted *Stoney Creek Trail*.

**4** Veer left, following the level bush track away from the signpost. As you climb, the vegetation becomes much drier. You will again pass some boulders and a *Cabbage Tree Walk Trail* sign on your left, just before reaching the intersection at the end of the Banksia picnic area. Facilities include tables, pit toilets, BBQ fire places, bins and tank water.

**5** Walk across the picnic area and pass around the gate, into the car park. You are now back at waypoint 1.

## Central Coast environment – the Cabbage Tree Palm

The Cabbage-Tree Palm is a tall, slender palm growing up to about 25 metres in height and 35 cm diameter. It is found in moist open forest, often in swampy sites and on margins of rainforests or near the sea. These trees are widely spread along the New South Wales coast, extending north into Queensland and south to eastern Victoria, growing further south than any other native Australian palm.

# 28 Somersby Falls

Starting from the Somersby Falls picnic area, this walk follows the picturesque series of waterfalls along Floods Creek. The picnic area provides gas barbeques, picnic tables, toilets (including wheelchair accessible) and ample parking, and this walk could easily be part of a family day out in the area. The main falls are approximately 8 metres high and are best viewed after rain. Note that this walk is in Brisbane Water National Park and an entry fee applies for cars driving in.

## At a glance

**Grade:** Medium

**Time:** 20 mins

**Distance:** 400 m return

**Ascent/descent:** 40 metres ascent/ descent

**Conditions:** The waterfalls are most spectacular after rain.

**Getting there:**
**Car:** Drive along Somersby Falls Rd to find the signposted entrance to Brisbane Water National Park; $7 vehicle fee (per 24 hrs); gates close at 5pm

**GPS of start/end:** -33.4011, 151.2701

Somersby Falls

## Walk directions

**1** From the information board at the lower end of the picnic area, follow the *To the Falls* sign down the stone, then timber stairs. At the bottom of the timber staircase, you will come to an intersection with a short path leading to the 1st Fall Lookout.

**2** From here turn right and follow the flat path down a few steps, keeping the fence to the left, to reach the 1st Falls Lookout. After retracing your steps, follow the stone stairs further down the hill. The track guides you through some pleasant bush, past a metal arrow post to come to a faint 'T' intersection with a dirt track on the left.

**3** From the bottom of the stone steps, turn right and follow the main track down the timber steps. You will soon come to a 'Y' intersection with a *Top Falls/Bottom Falls* sign.

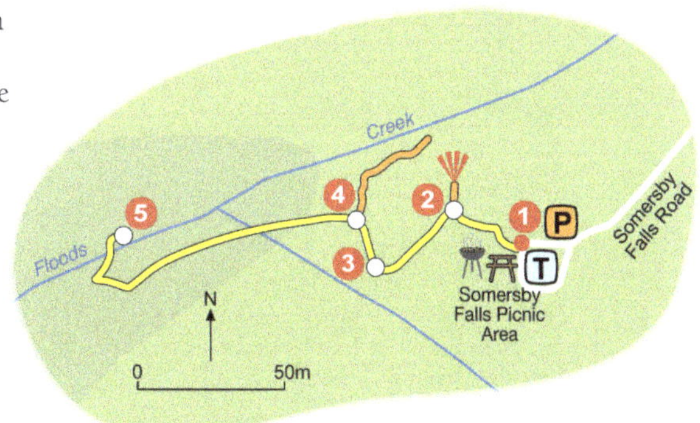

**4** Follow the *Bottom Falls* sign down the hill. The track soon leads you along a sandstone platform (passing a metal arrow) and down some stone steps to come to a timber platform. Follow the platform, head down a few further stairs and at the bottom, turn sharply right and follow the stone steps down to the creek (on the way, the track passes over a slippery unfenced rock ledge – take care here). Just before the creek, there is a *No Track Beyond This Point* sign. The steps then lead to the rock platform at the base of the falls – which can also be quite slippery. The bottom Somersby Falls tumble down through mossy boulders to the rock platform, and are particularly spectacular after rain.

**5** Return the way you came.

## Walk variation
## Side trip to Top Falls

From point 4 veer right, following the *Top Falls* sign to the rock platform. This can be slippery and there is an unfenced cliff - so take care. Once on the rock platform, turn right to visit the falls, where water cascades steeply down the jagged rock face onto a large rock platform. The water continues its flow across the rock and over another ledge to form the 'bottom falls', then on down to Mooney Mooney Creek. Retrace your steps back to point 4.

# 29 Popran Creek from Peats Ridge Road

A short but very steep walk down to a lovely spot beside Popran Creek. The area around the creek crossing is great to explore, with rainforest-covered tributaries adding to the scenery.

### At a glance

**Grade:** Medium

**Time:** 1 hr 15 mins

**Distance:** 2.5 km return

**Ascent/descent:** 190 metres ascent/descent

**Conditions:** Any season.

**Getting there:**
**Car:** Drive to a small car park, about 100 metres along an unmarked management trail on the western side of Peats Ridge Rd, about one kilometre south of Brieses Rd

**GPS of start/end:** -33.382, 151.2242

## Walk directions

1 From the car park, go around the gate and follow the management trail. This follows the path of an underground pipeline and there are numerous marker posts and other paraphernalia along here. The walk passes through or around another gate and comes to an intersection marked with a Popran National Park signpost. Continue straight ahead from the intersection, following the management trail down the hill. This section of the walk descends very steeply through the forest before arriving at Popran Creek.

2 The valley here at Popran Creek is deep, shaded and moist, with patches of rainforest and some tributaries to explore. Return the way you came.

# 30 Ironbark Road to Glenworth Valley

This walk, mostly in Popran National Park, passes through a variety of scenery and views. The early part of the walk, along a ridge top, is through relatively dry forest with some impressive views, while the steep descent to Glenworth Valley is through moist, fern filled forest. There is also an optional side trip for some good views from Mount Olive. If you can organise a lift from Glenworth Valley, that would save the walk back up the hill, maybe even provide enough time for a horse ride. The café at Glenworth Valley is open on weekends.

## At a glance

**Grade:** Hard

**Time:** 4 hrs 15 mins

**Distance:** 10 km return

**Ascent/descent:** 490 metres ascent/descent

**Conditions:** All seasons.

**Getting there:**
**Car:** From Wisemans Ferry Rd, drive about 6.8 km along Ironbark Rd – there is a parking area here with a NPWS *Popran Trail* signpost (if your car has reasonable ground clearance, you could drive further, to the Ironbark picnic area (point 2), and start the walk from there)

**GPS of start:** -33.3716, 151.1953

**GPS of Glenworth Valley:** -33.4026, 151.1931

## Walk directions

**1** Starting from the car park at the end of the *Pipeline Trail*, follow Ironbark Road south, ignoring the *Pipeline Trail* gate to the left. The gravel road passes between some houses with prominent private property signs so stick to the road along here. After 1.7 kilometres the track eventually comes to a car park and picnic area.

**2** From the car park, go around the gate and follow the management trail about 300 metres down the hill until you come to an intersection marked with Mt Olive and the *248 Trail*.

**3** Turn left at this intersection and follow the Mt Olive signpost along the bush track. After 120 metres you will reach an intersection with another bush track.

**4** Turn right at the intersection, following the bush track steeply down the hill, directly away from the top of Mount Olive (to summit Mount Olive, turn left at the intersection, following the bush track steeply up the hill for about 60 metres). Follow the bush track for a long distance, through a variety of terrain and vegetation. The first section of the walk is along, or close to, the ridgeline, offering scenic views. The later section of the walk drops, steeply at times, into Glenworth Valley and passes through more moist, fern covered forest.

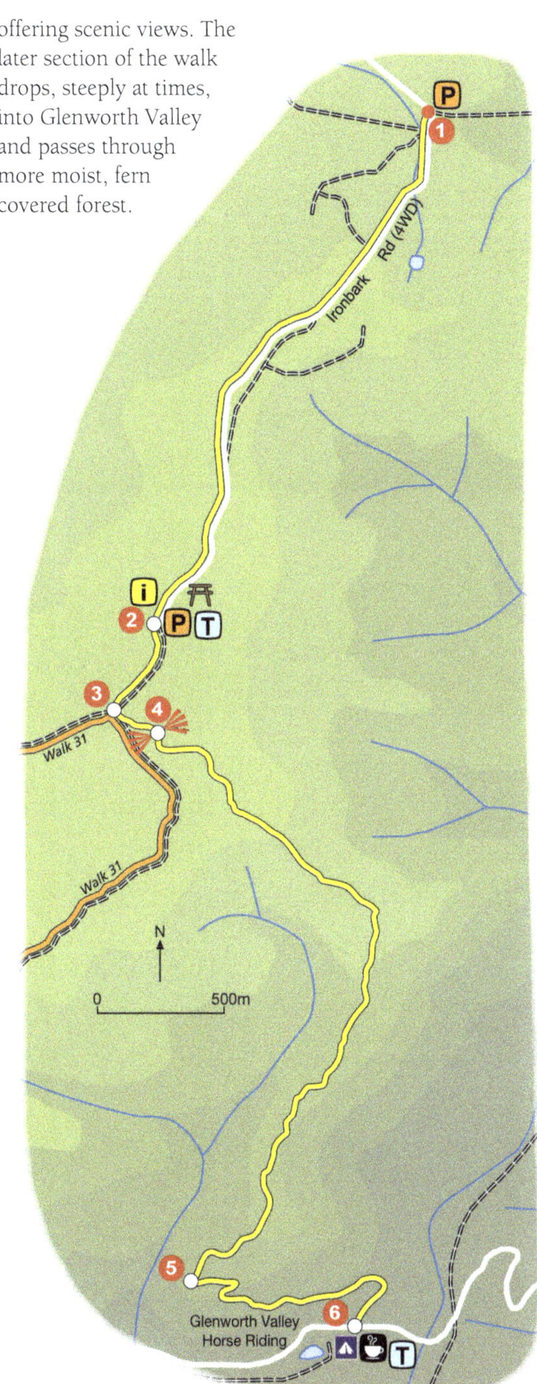

# 30 Ironbark Road to Glenworth Valley

**5** During the steep descent, take the sharp right fork beside a rock with a large 'capstone' to avoid a steeper section of the track. The scenery is beautiful on the descent. Ignore the track to the right when you pass through a gap in a fence, and follow the bush track straight ahead. You then come to an intersection with the Wilderness Trail horse riding trail on the edge of a large grassy clearing at the Glenworth Valley Horse Riding Centre. Continue down the hill and immediately turn to the right, following the track toward the clearly visible main buildings of the Glenworth Valley Horse Riding Centre.

**6** You will soon arrive at Popran Road beside the buildings. Return the way you came.

Glenworth Valley

# 31 Emerald Pool circuit from Ironbark Road

A great circuit walk in Popran National Park, to the beautiful Emerald Pool, this passes through a variety of vegetation and offers some expansive views along the way. It is well worth spending some time exploring Emerald Pool and around the creek. The optional side trips along the 248 trail and to Mt Olive add to the views on the walk.

### At a glance

**Grade:** Medium

**Time:** 4 hrs 15 mins

**Distance:** 10.8 km circuit

**Ascent/descent:** 350 metres ascent/descent

**Conditions:** All seasons. Limited shade. Emerald Pool is a great spot to cool off. Creek crossings may not be passable after rain.

**Getting there:**
**Car:** From Wisemans Ferry Rd, drive about 6.8 km along Ironbark Rd – there is a parking area here with a NPWS 'Popran Trail' signpost (if your car has reasonable ground clearance, you could drive further, to the Ironbark picnic area (point 2), and start the walk from there)

**GPS of start/end:** -33.3716, 151.1953

## Walk directions

**1** Starting from the car park at the end of the *Pipeline Trail*, follow Ironbark Road south, leaving the *Pipeline Trail* gate to the left. The gravel road passes between some houses with prominent private property signs so stick to the road along here. After about 1.5 kilometres you come to a car park and picnic area at the end of the road.

**2** From the car park, go around the gate and follow the management trail about 300 metres down the hill until you come to an intersection marked with *Mt Olive* and the *248 Trail*.

**3** Turn right and follow the *248 Trail* arrow. This meanders for a while and descends gently before passing through the signposted *Donovans Forest*. After climbing from here and meandering a little further, the trail arrives at the signposted intersection of the *Hominy Creek Trail* and the *248 Trail*.

**4** Veer left, following the *Hominy Creek Trail* arrow until arriving at the *No horses beyond this point* signpost, where the increasingly overgrown management trail becomes a bush track.

**5** Continue on, descending gently and passing through more swampy ground before dropping steeply to arrive at the intersection of the *Hominy Creek Track* and the *Emerald Pool* track, beside Hominy Creek.

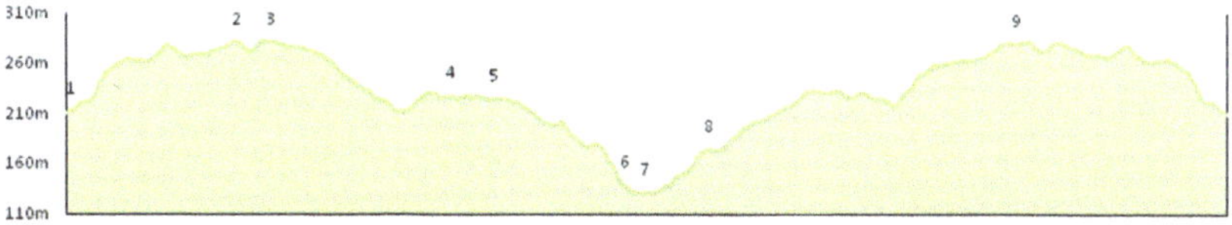

**6** Turn right, following the *Emerald Pool* arrow and keeping the creek to your left. You will find the Emerald Pool about 100 metres down this track. The pool is deep and has crystal clear water with an emerald green hue. There is a small cascade that falls into the pool, making it a great stop for lunch

7 Backtrack from the *Emerald Pool* for a short distance to the intersection at the creek crossing. Turn right, cross the creek, then follow the *Hominy Creek Track* up the hill. The walk climbs and meanders for a while before reaching the end of a management trail, signposted with *Hominy Creek Track* and *No horses beyond this point.*

8 Follow the management trail up the hill to the intersection with the *Mt Olive Trail* and veer left, following the *Car park 2.7 km* arrow. The walk climbs gently for some distance, offering views along the way, before arriving at an intersection with a bush track (signposted *Mt Olive*).

9 From the intersection, continue straight ahead, leaving the *Mt Olive* signpost on the right. After a very short distance, the trail arrives at an intersection signposted with *Mt Olive* and the *248 Trail* (you are now back at waypoint 3). Turn right and retrace your steps back to your car.

## Walk variation - 248 Trail

From waypoint 4, turn right at the intersection and follow the 248 Trail for about 600 metres, going up the gentle hill. The track ends at a large rocky outcrop, which can be explored and has some nice views. Be careful to avoid damaging some faint Aboriginal carvings on these rocks. Retrace your steps back to waypoint 4.

## Walk variation - Mount Olive

From waypoint 9, turn right at the intersection, following the Mt Olive signpost along the bush track. The walk continues for a while then veers left and follows the bush track steeply up the hill, soon arriving at the top of Mount Olive. The hill offers views in all directions from its peak, at which you can also find remnants of a couple of old trig points. Retrace your steps back to waypoint 9.

# Dharug National Park

I am not sure why, but this park really captures my imagination and I cannot help but be touched by its complex history and wildness. The walks chosen for this chapter help you explore some of this history and beauty. For the most part the first three walks follow the old roads and explore some well preserved heritage items, whilst still visiting some quiet remote places. Dharug National Park is a large reserve protecting steep rocky valleys, sandstone caves, diverse flora and fauna and the historic Old Great North Road. The history of the Old Great North Road could inspire a book of its own (and probably has!). Here you will find an opportunity to follow in the footsteps of the convicts who toiled to construct these trails that now provide access through some very rugged country.

Heading back many thousands of years further, the local Aboriginal people have long called this place home, and the park protects ancient and significant Aboriginal sites. Although rugged, this rich region provided many sandstone shelters, an abundance of food, water, and other materials for the traditional owners.

# 32 Dubbo Gully to Upper Mangrove Cemetery

While this walk does not actually enter Dharug National Park, it's an interesting stroll through McPherson State Forest and along Mangrove Creek Water Catchment reserve, with some great scenery along the way to the small, historic cemetery at Upper Mangrove. Evidence of Aboriginal activity in the area stretches back at least 5,000 years. Early European settlement here was concerned with timber and produce farming, before it also became established as a stop-off for travellers on the Great North Road.

## At a glance

**Grade:** Medium

**Time:** 3 hrs 15 mins

**Distance:** 7.2 km return

**Ascent/descent:** 450 metres ascent/descent

**Conditions:** All seasons

**Getting there:**

**Car:** Drive along Wisemans Ferry Rd to Mangrove Mountain, then about 4 km west on Waratah Rd and left into Dubbo Gully Rd – then drive about 450 m to a small parking area on the right

**GPS of start/end:** -33.293, 151.1512

Upper Mangrove Cemetery

## Walk directions

**1** Follow the management trail from the car park down the hill and around the gate, ducking under some tall rock overhangs. In about 2.5 kilometres you should reach the signposted intersection with the *Upper Mangrove Creek Rd* (just before a bridge). Continue across the longer bridge (leaving the shorter bridge with a gate to the right) and travel along the trail for some time, passing an old *134* sign to the right and a few old orange trees to the left.

**2** Soon after passing under some high voltage power lines, you arrive at the signposted historic cemetery. It was part of St Thomas' Church of England, was destroyed in the 2002 bushfires. Among others you will find the stone remembering Alfred and Amanda Andrews, who built Fairview homestead in 1922. Return the way you came.

210m
160m
110m
60m
10m

## Side Trip to Fairview homestead

From waypoint 2, continue straight ahead along the management trail and down the hill. Passing a swampy area to the right and a large grassy clearing to the left, you will reach a signposted intersection with *Donny's Track*. Continue straight ahead, leaving *Donny's Track* to the right, passing around a gate and, a little further, a wetland to the left, to find a gate and dirt trail on the right. Head around the gate and follow the driveway until you arrive at an old, abandoned house, 1.7 kilometres from waypoint 2. Retrace your steps back to the start of the walk.

## Central Coast history - Fairview

Fairview (550 Ten Mile Hollow Road) is a property with a homestead built in 1922 by Alfred Andrews. Though the homestead and adjoining slab hut are now fenced to protect them, the large corrugated iron shed on the south side is still open. The homestead was once a popular rest area for people travelling the North Road via the Simpson track. The home was privately owned until 1973 when Gosford City Council acquired the land to protect the catchment area. The home was then rented until 2002, when the tenants moved due to the threat of bushfires. The building is now in poor condition and the *Friends of Fairview* are exploring ways to save the building and restore the history of the valley.

# 33 Dubbo Gully and Ten Mile Hollow Circuit

This two day walk (or 10-hour day walk) follows several historic roads, now closed to traffic, and is a great way to explore the history and beauty of the area. Starting with a walk down Dubbo Gully and past an old cemetery, you will explore some old farms before coming to Simpsons Track and, up the hill, the Ten Mile Hollow Campsite. The next day, you will follow the Old Great North Road, visiting Clare's Bridge (second oldest bridge on mainland Australia) heading down Donny's track to return to the start via Dubbo Gully.

### At a glance

**Grade:** Hard

**Time:** 2 days

**Distance:** 24.3 km circuit

**Ascent/descent:** 1,120 metres ascent/descent

**Conditions:** Best on cooler days

**Getting there:**

**Car:** Drive along Wisemans Ferry Rd to Mangrove Mountain, then about 4 km west on Waratah Rd and turn left into Dubbo Gully Rd - drive to a small parking area about 450 m on the right.

**GPS of start/end:** -33.293, 151.1512

## Walk directions

**1** Follow *Dubbo Gully to Upper Mangrove Cemetery* walk number 32 to waypoint 2.

**2** Continue along the management trail down through the valley, passing a swampy area to the right and a large grassy clearing to the left. Soon you will reach a signposted intersection with *Donny's Track*.

**3** Veer left at the intersection, passing around a locked gate and another wetland before coming to a large gravelly clearing and intersection near a gate. For a side trip to Fairview Homestead, take the right branch around the gate and travel up the driveway to the abandoned house (see walk number 32 for more details on Fairview).

**4** Head along the main management trail past a grassy clearing and an old trail on the left to reach the *Heritage Road Wall & Culvert Protection* signpost. Allow some time to look at the sections of old road retaining wall along here. Keep walking along the old road past various clearings and a steel *Monitoring Well*. Soon after this, you head through another long clearing with the remains of an old wood-fenced cattle yard before crossing Ten Mile Hollow Creek. About 100 metres later, you will come across a clearing with a couple of boulders, *Convict Trail* plaque and a visitors' book (in the metal box at the back of the rock). About 25 metres past these plaques is the intersection with the Simpson Track, marked with a *National Park walkers* signpost.

**5** Turn right along the flat trail (the Simpson Track), heading further up the Ten Mile Hollow gully. After crossing a few creeks you enter denser

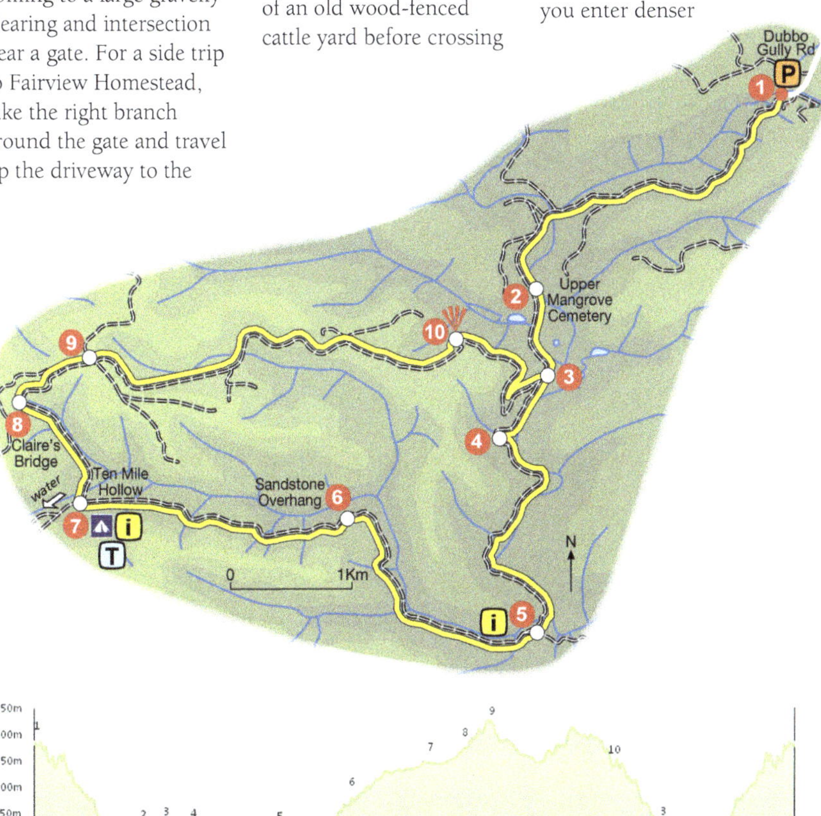

bush land and, about 1.7 kilometres from the large clearing, you reach Dharug National Park. About 750 metres up the trail you will come to the base of a large cliff with a couple of sandstone overhangs up the hill on the left. The cave has an outward sloping floor and is best viewed from the track.

Clare's Bridge

**6** Keep on Simpsons Track, winding up the hill for just over 2 kilometres before passing under some high-tension power lines in a large clearing. About 200 metres past this clearing, you come to the signposted intersection with the *Old Great North Road at Ten Mile Hollow* campsite, a former stockade for the convicts who built the road around 1830, and which can be a great spot for an overnight stay or lunch break. If the water tank here is empty you might find water in Ten Mile Hollow creek, not far north along the Old Great North Road, or in the tank provided at the Wat Buddha Dhamma, 600 metres south on the OGNR (remember to treat water before drinking).

**7** Take the sharp right at the intersection, following the *Clare's Bridge* sign along the OGNR. Cross the old timber base bridge (and Ten Mile Hollow Creek) and head around the gate. Walk along the overgrown old road for about 1 kilometre before circling around the white barricade to reach a clearing and signpost just before *Clare's Bridge*. This bridge is the most visually spectacular of those found along the Old Great North Road. The second oldest bridge on mainland Australia (the oldest being

Thomas James Bridge), it is built of sandstone blocks and has a wonderful, sweeping retaining wall.

Much work has been done by the National Parks and Wildlife Service and Gosford Council to restore the bridge.

**8** Cross the gully, keeping Clare's Bridge to the right. On the other side of the gully, the track rises to meet the old road again. About 500 metres on you will pass the Wat track on the left (signposted with 125,126 142-168), and another 250 metres will lead you to a large clearing and four-way intersection.

**9** Continue straight, following the *Donny's Track* sign downhill. The trail soon bends right and starts to flatten out, and at length crosses a wide gully and the often-dry creek. Wind up the hill past a few cuttings and under some power lines. About 300 metres after this you will pass the signposted 138 137 track on the left – keep on the main trail as it bends right and up the hill, continuing across a saddle and down the other side. After a couple of sharp bends you come to another right-hand bend and an unfenced rock platform with views into the valley; the informally named Donny's view.

**10** Continue downhill along the old road, around the base of some high-cut cliffs and a few rusty guard rails, until you reach a locked gate. Head around the locked gate and past the *Dharug National Park* sign. Keep walking between the two old fence posts, the sharp left-bend and two more old gate posts. Head down the hill to return to the intersection with the old Ten Mile Hollow Road and waypoint 3 (there is a sign pointing back up *Donny's Track*). From here turn left and retrace your steps 4.4 kilometres past the cemetery back to the start of the walk.

# 34 Devine's Hill and Finch's Line circuit

An intriguing walk with a mixture of historic remnants of the Old Great North Road and some beautiful views over the Hawkesbury River. Most of this walk follows parts of the convict-built road and a number of information signs along the way give a good insight into the construction and history of the road. Built between 1826 and 1836, the road formed a link between Sydney and the Hunter Valley. There are visible remnants of the original work in bridges, retaining walls and other structures along the way. The 'Convict Trail Project' has member groups involved in the conservation of historical remnants along the road (see www.convicttrail.org). The last section of the walk, along Wisemans Ferry Road, has some good views of the cliffs above. The historic Thomas James bridge, just before the end of the walk, is the oldest in-use bridge on mainland Australia.

## At a glance

**Grade:** Medium

**Time:** 4 hrs 30 mins

**Distance:** 9.9 km circuit

**Ascent/descent:** 550 metres ascent/descent

**Conditions:** All seasons

**Getting there:**

**Car:** The walk starts on Wisemans Ferry Rd, about 500m north west of the car ferry – there is a NPWS signpost marking *The Old Great North Road*

**GPS of start/end:** -33.3752, 150.9849

## Walk directions

1 From the car park on Wisemans Ferry Road, walk around the locked gate, passing an information sign, and follow the *Old Great North Road* sign up the hill. This section passes numerous cuttings and retaining walls built with convict labour. After a left-hand bend you will arrive at the signposted *Hangman's Rock*. The cave has some steps and a bench seat cut into it, and appears to have been built at the same time as the original road.

2 Continue from the cave, winding gently up the hill and passing another information sign indicating the probable site of a stockade to hold the "more troublesome convicts". A little further along you will pass around a gate and reach the intersection with old *Shepherd's Gully Road.* Veer right with the *Finch's Line 500m* arrow along the old road, travelling past an uncovered culvert display and information sign. About 300 metres further uphill you will find a signposted intersection.

# 34 Devine's Hill and Finch's Line circuit

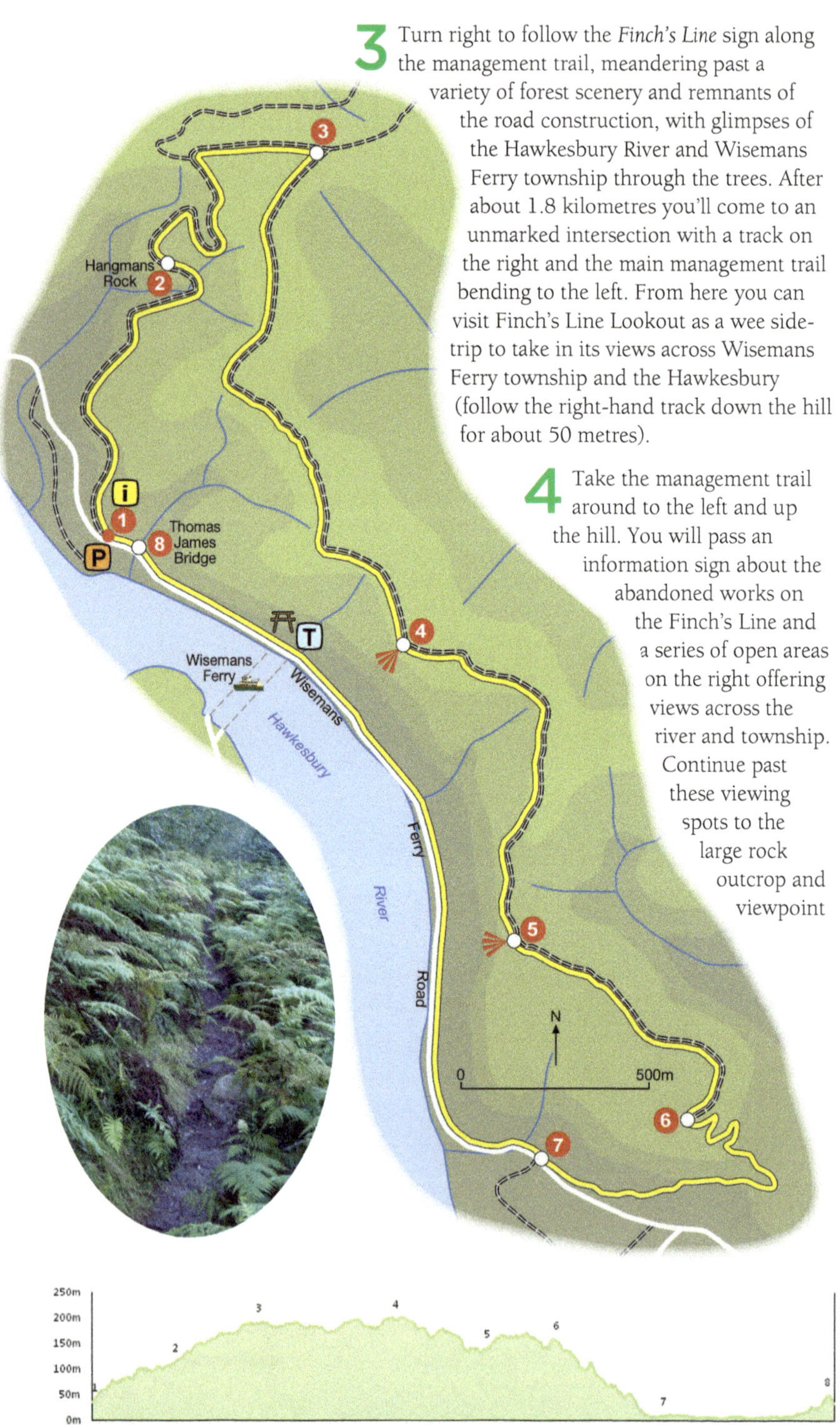


**3** Turn right to follow the *Finch's Line* sign along the management trail, meandering past a variety of forest scenery and remnants of the road construction, with glimpses of the Hawkesbury River and Wisemans Ferry township through the trees. After about 1.8 kilometres you'll come to an unmarked intersection with a track on the right and the main management trail bending to the left. From here you can visit Finch's Line Lookout as a wee side-trip to take in its views across Wisemans Ferry township and the Hawkesbury (follow the right-hand track down the hill for about 50 metres).

**4** Take the management trail around to the left and up the hill. You will pass an information sign about the abandoned works on the Finch's Line and a series of open areas on the right offering views across the river and township. Continue past these viewing spots to the large rock outcrop and viewpoint on the right, just as the trail bends to the left and heads away from the cliff line.

**5** Follow the management trail away from the cliff line as the trail switches to the other side of the ridge and offers some beautiful views back across the valley. After a reasonably steep drop you will arrive at a junction with a sign indicating that bikes must be walked.

**6** Take the left track as it zigzags down a steep hill, along the path of Finch's Line Road. After winding down the hill for just over a kilometre, you come to Wisemans Ferry Road, signposted with *Finch's Line Walking Track*

**7** Turn right along the road (immediately passing a noticeable sandstone gateway to the left), keeping the Hawkesbury River on your the left and views of the cliffs to the right. At length you will reach the northern end of the car ferry (Wisemans Ferry), signposted as the *Gosford Approach*. There are toilets here. About 600 metres past the ferry you will find the historic Thomas James Bridge, built by 'Road Party 25' during 1830 and named after the overseer.

**8** Cross the bridge and continue along the road for another 100 metres back to the car park and *The Old Great North Road* sign.

## Out and about - Wisemans Ferry

Both Wisemans Ferry village and the ferry itself are named after Solomon Wiseman, a former convict who received a land grant in the area and established the ferry service. The town is a popular day trip and weekend destination from Sydney and there are several good spots to eat, including bistros at the Wisemans Ferry Inn and Bowling club, plus takeaway food from Bush Bites Café. The Riverbend Restaurant can be found in the 'Retreat at Wisemans' for finer dining. The area has some great walking and interesting history surrounding the convict-built Old Great North Road.

# 35 11km Circuit

This circuit walk offers a lot of beautiful scenery and views. Although shorter than the name suggests (it's actually just over 8 km), it is a reasonably tough walk with some steep rocky sections. The route through the gullies and valleys are moist with lots of ferns, while the higher sections pass through drier forest. There are also some lovely cliffs and boulders to be seen at various points around the walk.

## At a glance

**Grade:** Hard

**Time:** 4 hrs 15 mins

**Distance:** 8.2 km circuit

**Ascent/descent:** 630 metres ascent/descent

**Conditions:** All seasons; creeks may be impassable after rain.

**Getting there:**

**Car:** Drive to the picnic area at the end of Mill Creek Rd off Wisemans Ferry Rd about 5.5 km east of Wisemans Ferry, signposted Mill Creek

**GPS of start/end:** -33.4008, 151.0478

## Finding the track

From the information signs at the Mill Creek picnic area, walk to the far end of the picnic area to find the start of the walk at the *Start/ Finish* signpost.

## Walk directions

**1** From the *Start/Finish* signpost, follow the track away from the picnic area and immediately take the right hand branch (the other track is the return leg of this walk). You will pass through a mix of dense vegetation and more open forest with some views and lots of grasstrees. After crossing a creek with wooden steps and a stone path, the track climbs more steeply before dropping back down to the signposted intersection of the *11km Walking Track* and *1.5km Grass Tree Circuit*.

**2** Follow the *11km Walking Track* arrow, climbing for a while past gully views and into a picturesque creek crossing marked with a small walker arrow. From here, climb steeply for a short distance before coming to a section with rock overhangs and boulders. The track then drops to another creek crossing, marked with a small walker sign on a boulder in the middle of the creek. Follow the walker arrow along the track, which has several steep climbs and plenty of great scenery. After some time you will pass a regenerating bush track to the right (marked with a walker post and old arrows on the trees) and cross a gully marked with arrows in both directions. After crossing another gully (unmarked), the track climbs very steeply to an

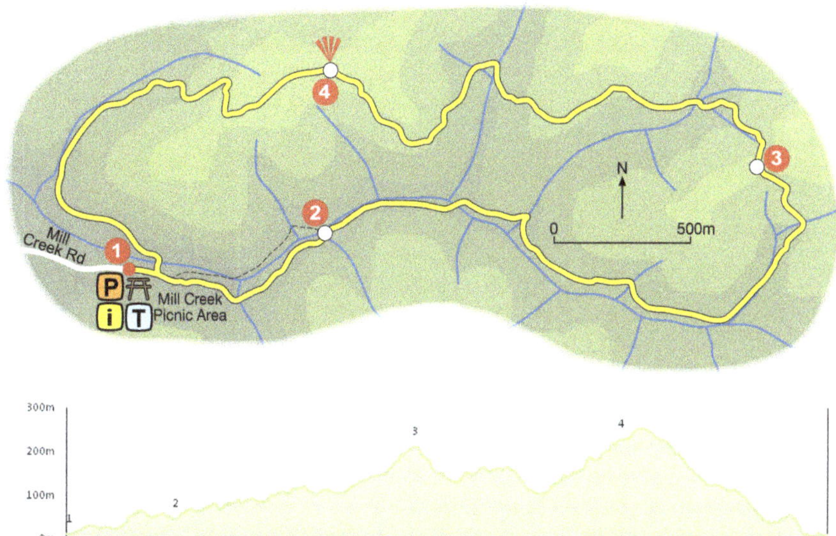

intersection at the top of the hill (the bush track to the right is very faint).

**3** Veer left, immediately bending to the right and dropping steeply down the hill. This section has some very steep sections as it drops and climbs through two gullies (and across a third minor tributary). At the top of a ridge there's an intersection on a small rock platform immediately after a track marker (the main track bends to the left here). There are minor tracks leading to a nearby (unfenced) rock platform with more views.

**4** Take the main trail, heading west and leaving the much larger rock platform to the right. You will soon pass a track marker on the left before climbing up the ridge line and down the other side. Descending steeply, you'll pass numerous track markers and eventually drop into the more shaded and moist lower part of the valley. At length cross a wooden bridge and climb some steps, arriving back at the Mill Creek Picnic area.

# 36 Grass Tree Circuit

The Grasstree is one of the icons of the Australian bush. It is a very slow growing plant, with the trunk typically only growing about one cm per year, and they can grow and survive for several hundred years. Travelling along the valley through a range of dry and wet forest, this walk offers some great views and plenty of grasstrees along the way to complement the landscape. The creek crossings are picturesque and the optional side trip adds some striking rock overhangs, giving a taste of the scenery on the longer '11km Circuit' walk (walk number 35).

## At a glance

**Grade:** Medium

**Time:** 1 hr

**Distance:** 1.7 km circuit

**Ascent/descent:** 110 metres ascent/descent

**Conditions:** All seasons; creeks may be impassable after rain

**Getting there:**

**Car:** Drive to the picnic area at the end of Mill Creek Rd off Wisemans Ferry Rd about 5.5 km east of Wisemans Ferry, signposted Mill Creek

**GPS of start/end:** -33.4008, 151.0478

## Finding the track

Walk from the information signs at the Mill Creek picnic area to the far end of the picnic area to find the start of the walk at the *Start/ Finish* signpost.

## Walk directions

**1** From the *Start/Finish* signpost, follow the track away from the picnic area and immediately take the right hand branch (the other track is the return leg of this walk). You will pass through a mix of dense vegetation and more open forest with some views and lots of grasstrees. After crossing a creek with wooden steps and a stone path, the track climbs more steeply before dropping back down to the signposted intersection of the *11km Walking Track* and *1.5km Grass Tree Circuit*.

**2** Turn left down the hill, walking immediately down some steps and across the creek. Soon after this, the track crosses a smaller gully and meanders for a while through the moist forest before crossing the main creek again. Hike through some drier forest to arrive back at the signposted track head at the end of the Mill Creek picnic area.

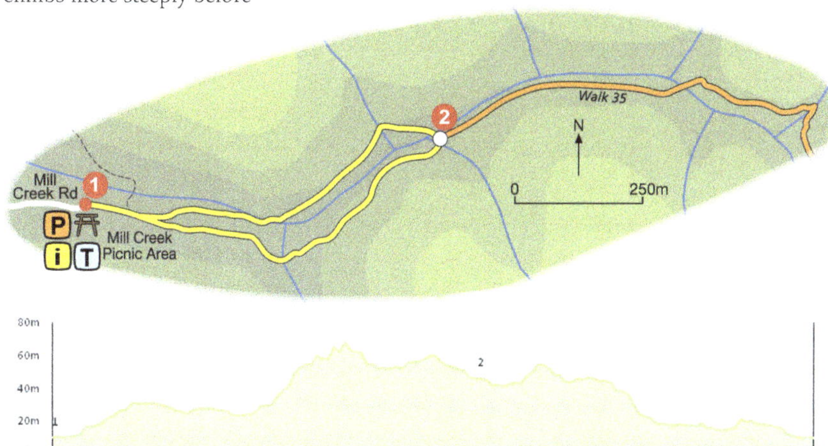


### Side Trip to 11km Big Tree creek crossing

From waypoint 2, follow the *11km Walking Track* arrow along the track. You will climb for a while before dropping to a creek crossing marked with a small walker arrow. From here, climb steeply up to a section with rock overhangs and boulders. Walk on, dropping to another creek crossing marked with a small walker sign on a boulder in the middle of the creek, beneath a huge tree with impressive roots draping over the rocks. Retrace your steps the 800 metres back to waypoint 2 (then turn right).

Mannering Lake
Wyee Rd
Newcastle Fwy
Pacific Hwy
Colonga Lake
LAKE MUNMORAH
Munmorah State Conservation Area
Lake Munmorah
Central Coast Hwy
BLUE HAVEN
SAN REMO
Motorway Link
Elizabeth Bay Dr
CHARMHAVEN
BUFF POINT
BUDGEWOI
LAKE HAVEN
Lake Budgewoi
ONGARRAH
GOROKAN
Main Rd
KANWAL
TOUKLEY
NORAVILLE
WYONGAH
TUGGERAWONG
Tuggerah Lake
NORAH HEAD
Wyrrabalong National Park
Wilfred Barrett Dr
N
0
5km
KILLARNEY VALE
SHELLY BEACH
BAY VILLAGE
NIAGARA PARK
LISAROW
BATEAU BAY
Tumbi Rd
WYOMING
FORRESTERS BEACH
Katandra Reserve
WAMBERAL
GOSFORD
SPRINGFIELD
ERINA HEIGHTS
Willoughby Rd
Ocean View Dr
Terrigal Dr
ERINA
TERRIGAL
Avoca Dr
GREEN POINT
PICKETTS VALLEY
Kincumber Recreation Reserve
Brisbane Water
KINCUMBER
AVOCA
YATTALUNGA
Faunce St
Erina St E
William St
Albany St Nth
Donnison St
Rumbalara Reserve
Dolly Ave
Start of walk 9
Mann St
Henry Parry Dr
Bayview Av
Lushington St
Wells St
Frederick St
Central Coast Hwy
1
2
3
4
5
6
7
8
9
10
11

SOMERSBY
Popran National Park
Peats Ridge Rd
29
28
26
27
Strickland State Forest
Fwy
Wisemans Ferry Rd
Sydney Newcastle
Rd
Manns
GOSFOR
WEST GOSFORD
Pacific Hwy
24 25
KARIONG
CALGA
Newcastle Fwy
Pacific Hwy
Mooney Mooney Creek
MT WHITE
Sydney
Brisbane Water National Park
23
Woy Woy Rd
20
21
TASCOTT
Brisbane Water Dr
Brisbane Water
KOOLEWONG
WOY WOY
WONDABYNE
22
HORSFIELD BAY
BLACKWALL
ETTALONG BEACH
West St
UMINA BEACH
17
PEARL BEACH
COGRA BAY
MOONEY MOONEY
Long Island
Dangar Island
BROOKLYN
19
Ferry Route
LITTLE WOBBY
PATONGA
18
Hawkesbury River
N
0
2k

EMPIRE BAY
BENSVILLE
MACMASTERS BEACH
DALEYS POINT
Maitland Bay Dr
Empire Bay Dr
BOOKER BAY
TALONG EACH
Scenic Rd
BOUDDI
The
Bouddi National Park
16 15
13
WAGSTAFFE
HARDYS BAY
KILLCARE HEIGHTS
14
PRETTY BEACH
KILLCARE
Maitland Bay
12
Box Head
N
0 2km

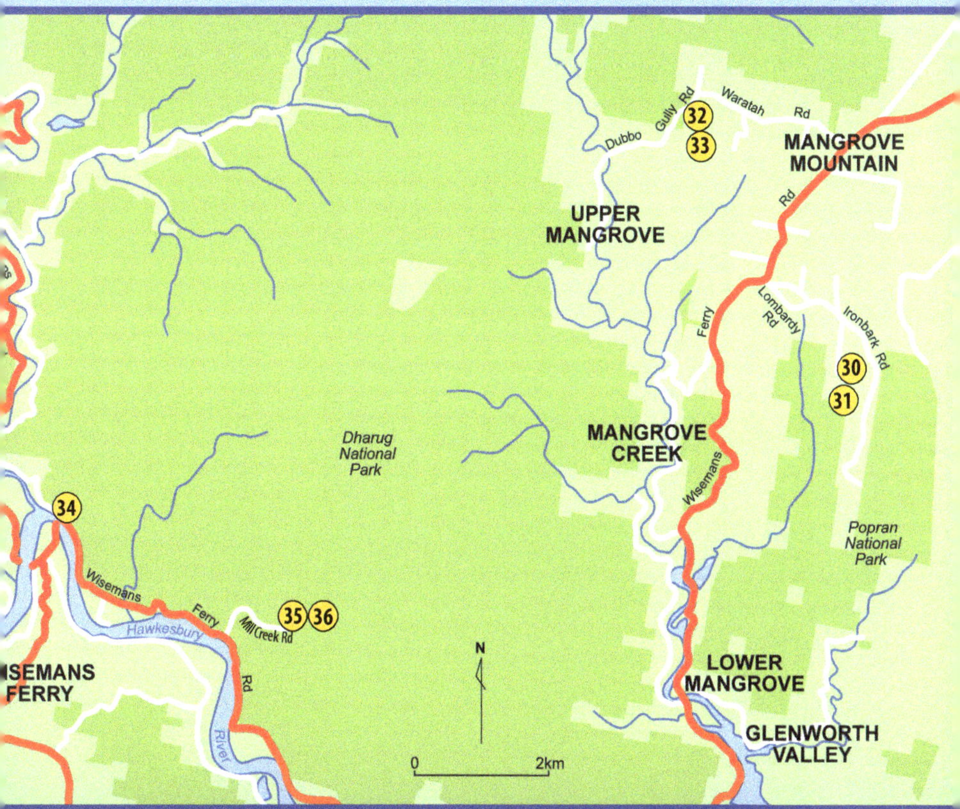

Waratah Rd
Gully Rd
Dubbo
32
33
MANGROVE MOUNTAIN
Rd
UPPER MANGROVE
Lombardy Rd
Ironbark Rd
Ferry
30
31
Dharug National Park
MANGROVE CREEK
Wisemans
Popran National Park
34
Wisemans Ferry Rd
35 36
Mill Creek Rd
Hawkesbury River
N
SEMANS FERRY
LOWER MANGROVE
GLENWORTH VALLEY
0 2km

# Navigation and staying found

Good navigation will help you have a safer and more enjoyable journey. The notes and maps will help, but you will still need to pay attention and be able to deal with changes.

For longer and harder walks, **carry a topographic map and compass** - you will need them. You can print more detailed topographical maps for each of these walks from wildwalks.com but it is also still worth carrying a 1:25,000 scale map of the larger area just in case. The following LPMA sheet maps cover the walks in this book: Broken Bay (91301N), Catherine Hill Bay (92314S), Cowan (91304N), Gosford (91312S), Gunderman (91313S), Lower Portland (90312S), Mangrove (91313N), St Albans (90312N), Toukley (92313N), Wyong (91312N).

A GPS is a helpful tool for finding your location and other useful info. Generally GPS still do not have detailed maps on them, but the co-ordinates can be useful when using maps marked with grids or when calling for help. A GPS is another tool and like compasses they have their limits.

**Don't leave the main track**, even if you are concerned that you're no longer on the correct track. 'Bush-bashing' to try to find your way is hard work, very slow and dangerous. If you feel you have gone the wrong way, stop, look at the maps and read the notes. It is often helpful to backtrack to the last place where you knew you were on track. If you see someone, swallow your pride and ask for help; you might make a new friend.

In the unlikely event you find yourself really lost, then stop and stay put on a track. Call for help and make yourself comfortable, visible and heard. If your phone does not work, remember that you have told someone responsible where you were going, and when you are due back. Trust that they will raise the alarm. You wandering about is only likely to make a search harder. Even if your phone is out of range try sending an SMS when holding the phone above your head. Sometimes a message will get through even when calls cannot. If sending an SMS please, send it to someone who will act (neither 112 nor 000 accept SMS's). Any message must be clear, with information about what help you need and where you are. If you have tried all reasonable means of getting help, and you feel your welfare is at risk then you can use your PLB. Whatever means you use to raise help, it will probably take hours (or longer); conserve your energy, keep warm, dry and get comfortable.

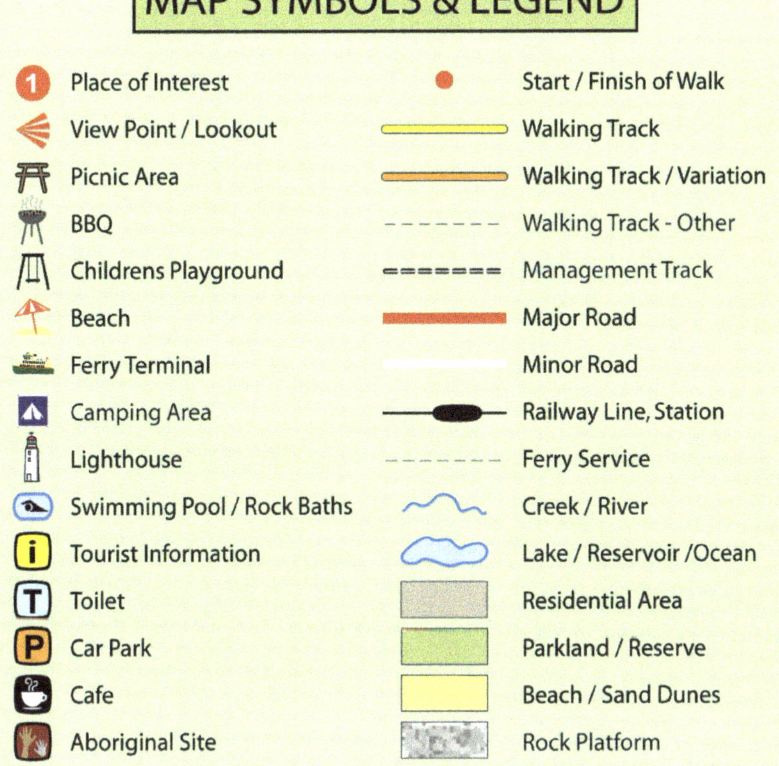
MAP SYMBOLS & LEGEND
Place of Interest
View Point / Lookout
Picnic Area
BBQ
Childrens Playground
Beach
Ferry Terminal
Camping Area
Lighthouse
Swimming Pool / Rock Baths
Tourist Information
Toilet
Car Park
Cafe
Aboriginal Site
Start / Finish of Walk
Walking Track
Walking Track / Variation
Walking Track - Other
Management Track
Major Road
Minor Road
Railway Line, Station
Ferry Service
Creek / River
Lake / Reservoir /Ocean
Residential Area
Parkland / Reserve
Beach / Sand Dunes
Rock Platform

# Index


11km (Mill Creek) Circuit, 156-159
248 Trail, 141

## A-B

Arboretum Loop Trail, 121-122
Bellbird Trail, 120-123
Birdie Beach, 13, 15
Bongon Lagoon, 14
Bouddi Coastal Walk, 80-83
Bouddi National Park, 65-83
Box Head, 66-68
Brisbane Water National Park, 85-117, 128-131
Brooklyn, 92, 93
Engravings, 107-109
Bullimah Outlook, 69-42
Bulls Hill Quarry, 100
Bundilla Lookout, 115
Bush Street Reserve, 17

## C

Cabbage Tree Loop, 124-126
Cabbage Tree Palm, 127
Casuarina Track, 37, 39
Charles Darcy Roberts, 71
Charles Kingsford Smith sculpture, 41, 47
Charles Sturt sculpture, 38, 39, 50
Clare's Bridge, 150
Croppy Point, 93

## D-E

Devines Hill and Finch's Line Circuit, 152-155
Dharug National Park, 148-163
Donny's Track, 151
Dubbo Gully and 10-mile Hollow Circuit, 148-151
Dubbo Gully to Upper Mangrove Cemetery, 144-147
Emerald Pool Circuit, 138-141
engravings, Aboriginal, 107-109, 111
Engravings, Bulgandry, 107-109
Eve Williams Memorial Oval, 88

## F-G

Fairview homestead, 146
Finch's Line, 152-155
Flannel Flower Track, 40-42
Frazer Beach, 12, 14
Geebung Track, 12
Gerrin Point Circuit, 73-77
Girrakool Loop, 110-113
Girrakool Picnic Area, 111, 115
Glenworth Valley, 134, 136
Gosford to Lisarow, 48-53
Grass Tree Circuit, 160-161
Grass Tree Track, 12, 14
Great North Walk, 88, 89, 116

## H-K

Hawkesbury River, 92, 93
Headland Nature Trail, 17
Illoura Lookout, 115
Ironbark and Flannel Flower Circuit, 40-42
Ironbark Road to Glenworth Valley, 134-137
John Eyre sculpture, 51
John Eyre, 53
John 'Jack' Higgs, 110
Kariong Brook, 102-103
Katandra Reserve Explorer, 54-59
Katandra Reserve, 51-59
Killcare Heights (Marie Byles) Lookout, 73
Kincumber to Terrigal, 60-63

## L-M

Lillypilly Loop Trail, 24, 26-28
Little Beach, 78-79
Little Wobby to Woy Woy, 92-97

Maitland Bay Information Centre, 69, 70, 74
Maitland Beach, 82
Marie Byles (Killcare Heights) Lookout, 73
Marie Byles, 73
Matthew Flinders sculpture, 41, 47
McPherson State Forest, 144-145
Merchant Mariners Memorial, 17
Mill Creek picnic area, 156, 157, 158, 160, 161
Mount Wondabyne, 95, 98-101
Mt Ettalong, 86-87
Mt Olive, 135, 140, 141
Munmorah Coast Track, 12-15

## N-P

Norah Head Lighthouse Loop, 16-19
Nurrunga Picnic Area, 41, 42, 44-47
Old Great North Road, 144, 148, 150-151, 152-154
Ouraka Point Loop, 36-39
Patonga to Pearl Beach, 88-91
Pearl Beach, 91
Pearl Caves, 90
Phil Houghton Suspension Bridge, 116
Piles Creek Circuit, 114-117
Piles Creek, 112-113, 114-117
Pindar Cave, 104-106
Pindar Lookout, 105
Pindar Pool, 106
Pindar Waterfall, 106
Popran Creek from Peats Ridge Road, 132-133
Popran National Park, 132-141
Putty Beach & camping area, 76, 77, 83

## R

Rainforest walk to Nurrunga, 44-47
Red Ochre Beach, 13
Redgum Trail, 22-25
Rocky Ponds, 92
Rumbalara Environmental Education Centre, 36, 49
Rumbalara Reserve, 36-51
Rumbalara sculptures, 39

## S

Seymour Pond, 55-56
Simpson's Track, 150
Snapper Point, 15
Somersby Falls, 128-131
Spring Beach, 94
SS Maitland, 80, 82, 83
St Johns Lookout & picnic area, 52, 59
Staples Lookout to Kariong Brook Falls, 102-103
Staples Lookout to Mount Wondabyne Circuit, 98-101
Strickland Falls and Cabbage Tree Loop, 124-127
Strickland Forest, 120-126

## T-Y

Ten Mile Hollow, 148-151
Thomas James Bridge, 152, 155
Thommo's Loop, 102-103
Timber Beach, 15
Tuggerah Lake, 22-24, 26-28
Upper Mangrove Cemetary, 144, 145
Vera Murdoch, 110
Warrah Lookout, 88, 89
Wiseman's Ferry, 155
Woy Woy, 97
Wybung Head, 12, 15
Wyrrabalong Coast Walking Track, 29-32
Wyrrabalong National Park, 22-24, 26-32
Yaruga Picnic Area, 50

# About the authors and Wildwalks

The walks in this book have been diligently documented by the people at Wildwalks. A special thanks to Ian Morrison, our first staff member, for helping lay the foundation.

**Matt McClelland**

Having developed a love for wild places through the Scouts, Matt established Wildwalks to share this passion with others. For this book, Matt has documented walks in Dharug NP, Brisbane Water NP, Munmorah SCA, Katandra Reserve and Kincumber Mountain.

**Kieran Babich**

A keen outdoors man, who holds a Bachelor of Applied Science (Ecotourism), Kieran is passionate about kayaking and walking. Kieran documented the walks in Bouddi NP for this book.

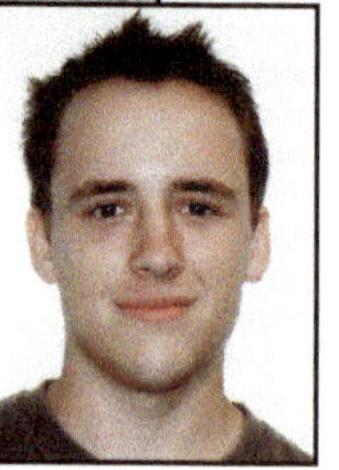

**Peter Buckle**

Peter is a keen walker and an unassuming fellow. Peter loves putting on his pack, grabbing a camera and spending days exploring long stretches of tracks. For this book, Peter documented many of the walks in Brisbane Water NP.

**Craig McClelland**

A keen traveller, photographer and computer nerd, Craig joined the Wildwalks team on a 3-month contract. Craig helped to improve the way we record information on walks, and for this book documented walks in Dharug NP, Wyrrabalong NP, Popran NP, Strickland SF, Rumbalara Reserve and at Norah Head.

**About Wildwalks**

Wildwalks is a small team of professional bushwalkers, dedicated to making bushwalking more accessible and safer for our community. At www.wildwalks.com you will find useful information on hundreds of walks around NSW, including track notes, photos, walk grades, walking times, terrain profiles and more. Our track notes are frequently upgraded, and there is up-to-date information on weather forecasts, fire ratings and park closures. There are also printable versions of track notes that include topographical maps. You may be surprised to discover how many more walks there are near you. Please visit www.wildwalks.com to leave feedback on your walk, and read about other people's experiences.


# Acknowledgements

I would like to first acknowledge the traditional owners of these lands, both past and present.

Thank you to the people at NSW NPWS (www.npws.nsw.gov.au) who are dedicated to protecting our state's most beautiful, significant and natural places. In particular I would like to thank Sarah Brookes (Dharug NP) for being so diligent in answering many of my strange questions.

A big thanks to the people of Forests NSW, Gosford City council, Glenworth Valley, and Broken Bay Sport and Rec Centre (in particular Matt Van Dorst). Also thanks to the volunteers at Convict Trail (www.convicttrail.org), in particular Elizabeth Roberts.

It is a great privilege to stand on the shoulders of many other authors, and a special thanks must go to Anthony Dunk for his generosity and his book "Discovering Gosford's Bushland on Foot".

To the people at Woodslane, thanks for your continued commitment to quality. A special thanks to Andrew Swaffer who guided me through the book publishing process. Coral Lee, thanks for lending your great eye for design, the book looks wonderful. Thanks also to Tony Fakira, the cartographer, for the great maps.

To my family and my family in-law, thank you for your support and love. To my wife Fiona who encourages me always, even when I quit my corporate job to chase a dream. And of course, to the two cutest and coolest kids, Eric and Laura, thanks for the joy.

# Woodslane Press

*Best Bush & Coastal Walks of the Central Coast* is just one of a growing series of outdoor guides from Sydney publishers Woodslane Press. To browse through other titles available from Woodslane Press, visit www.woodslane.com.au. If your local bookshop does not have stock of a Woodslane Press book, they can easily order it for you. In case of difficulty please contact our customer service team on 02 8445 2300 or info@woodslane.com.au.

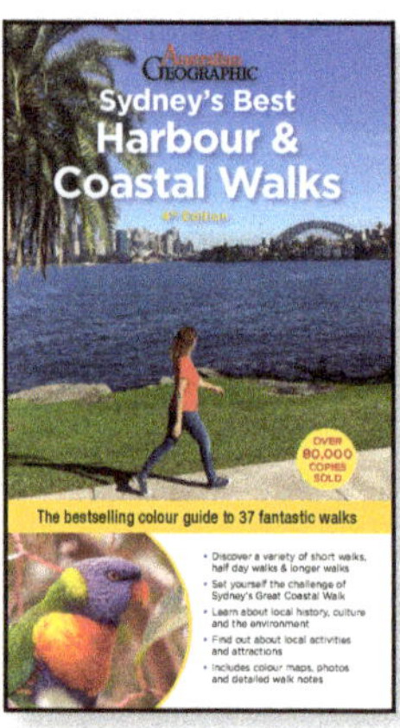

Titles include:

**Sydney's Best Harbour & Coastal Walks**

$32.99
ISBN: 9781925403664

---

**The Great North Walk**

$32.99
ISBN: 9781921874215

---

**Sydney's Best Bush, Park & City Walks**

$32.99
ISBN: 9781925403572

---

**Blue Mountains Best Bushwalks**

$32.99
ISBN: 9781925403299

The Six Foot Track

$19.99

ISBN: 9781921874239

Best Walks of The Illawarra

$32.99

ISBN: 9781925868456

Best Walks of the Southern Highlands

$32.99

ISBN: 9781925868111

Best Walks of the Shoalhaven

$32.99

ISBN: 9781925403558

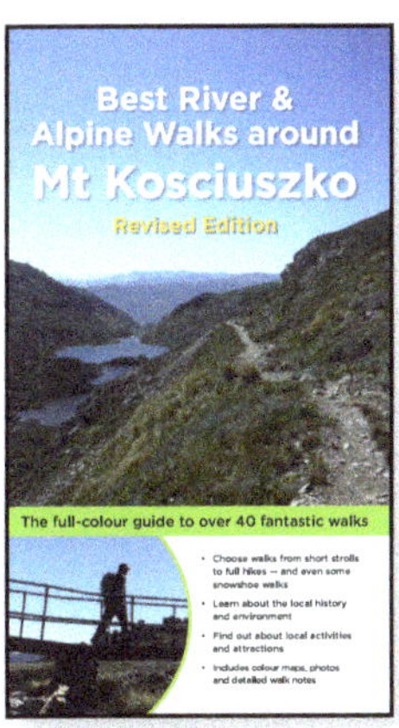


Best River & Alpine Walks around Mt Kosciuszko

$32.99

ISBN: 9781921606045

Canberra's Best Bush, Park & City Walks

$32.99

ISBN: 9781922131492

# Your thoughts appreciated!

We do hope that you are enjoying using this book, but we know that nothing in this world is perfect and your suggestions for improving on this edition would be much appreciated.

Your name ____________________

Your address or email address ____________________

____________________

____________________

Your contact phone number ____________________

Are you a resident or visitor to Central Coast? ____________________

What you most liked about this book ____________________

____________________

____________________

What you least liked about this book ____________________

____________________

____________________

Which is your favourite walk featured in this book?

____________________

Which walk wasn't featured but you think should have been included?

____________________

Would you like us to keep you informed of other Woodslane books?
If so: are you interested in:

- ☐ walking
- ☐ visiting natural & historic sites
- ☐ picnicking
- ☐ cycling
- ☐ general outdoor activities
- ☐ activities in Central Coast region only
- ☐ activities in NSW
- ☐ activities around Australia

What others books would you like to see in this series?

____________________

____________________

**Woodslane Pty Ltd • 10 Apollo Street • Warriewood • NSW 2102 • Email: info@woodslane.com.au**

www.ingramcontent.com/pod-product-compliance
Ingram Content Group UK Ltd.
Pitfield, Milton Keynes, MK11 3LW, UK
UKHW062257290726
14090UKWH00017B/738

9 781921 606854